Australian

SPIDERS

in colour

by RAMON MASCORD

Atrax robustus
Sydney Funnel-web Spider

REED

CONTENTS

First published 1970
Reprinted 1977, 1979, 1983, 1989, 1991, 1993

REED
a part of Wm. Heinemann Australia
Level 9, North Tower, Railway St.
Chatswood NSW 2067

National Library of Australia
Cataloguing in Publication Data
Mascord, Ramon.
    Australian spiders in colour.
    Includes index.
    ISBN 0 7301 0291 2.
    1. Spiders – Australia. I. Title.
595.4′4′0994

Printed in Singapore For
Imago Productions (F.E.) Pte. Ltd.

INTRODUCTION

THE STUDY OF AUSTRALIA'S SPIDERS has suffered from apathy and neglect. Many of our spiders are but names to the scientists of other countries, and some are practically unknown to our own arachnologists. The last checklist on the subject was published as long aso as 1911, by William J. Rainbow. Most of the type specimens are in overseas museums and inaccessible to our students.

This small book aims to interest and enlighten the public and the serious student on some of our fairly common species, by means of colour photography and a simple but informative text.

In the fifty-seven years that have elapsed since the issue of Rainbow's 1911 checklist the scientific names of many species have been changed, and some species have been placed in different genera. The species here illustrated have been given the names by which they are known today, and have also been given the common name where there is one in use. Where more than one common name is used, the one which has the most widespread usage has been selected.

Many hitherto undescribed species are still being found, and many of the earlier-named species are being rediscovered.

It is the author's wish that this book may stimulate yet new discoveries in the world of Australian spiders.

External Anatomy

The body of a spider consists of two basic sections which are connected by a thin pedicel or tube. The anterior or front section is called the cephalothorax or prosoma, and the posterior or back section the abdomen or opisthosoma. The cephalothorax bears the eyes, mouthparts and legs, while the abdomen bears the respiratory openings, reproductive and digestive systems, and the spinning apparatus, or spinnerets.

Cephalothorax

The cephalothorax is unsegmented, and is covered on the dorsal or upper surface by a hard shield which is called the carapace. The carapace usually has a conspicuous depression or pit, known as the thoracic fovea. From this pit radiate four furrows. The front pair depict the outline of the head from the thorax, and are called cervical grooves. The margin between the front row of eyes and the front edge of the carapace is called the clypeus.

At the front edge of the carapace are the eyes, known as simple ocelli. The eyes usually number eight, though some families have six. The eyes are of taxonomic importance, for their relative sizes, position, and spacing often define a species. The eyes are usually referred to as: anterior medians or front middle (AME); anterior laterals or front outside (ALE); posterior medians or back middle (PME); and posterior laterals or back outside (PLE). The area contained by the AME and PME is called the median ocular area (MOE).

Chelicerae

The chelicerae are the foremost appendages of the cephalothorax. These are used for the capture and killing of prey, for digging burrows and for defence purposes. They are made up of two segments, the stout basal segment, or paturon, and the smaller curved segment, or fang. When not in use the fangs fold away into a groove. If present, the teeth on the front margin are called promarginal teeth, and those on the back margin are called retromarginal teeth. These teeth are important in classification.

The opening of the poison duct is at the tip of the fang. In mygalomorph spiders (Trap-door and Funnel-web spiders), the fangs move up and down and the chelicerae are known as par-axial. Most other spiders have what is known as di-axial chelicerae, which move sideways in a pincer-like movement.

Pedipalp

The pedipalpi are usually called palps and differ in male and female spiders. On immature males and females of a species, the palps are similar to a smaller leg with six segments, whereas the legs have seven segments. In mature males the tarsal segment is usually enlarged and complicated, as this is the genital organ of the male spider. The palps are situated at the front and on either side of the cephalothorax, between the chelicerae and the first pair of legs. From the cephalothorax outwards the palp segments are: coxa, trochanter, femur, patella, tibia, and tarsus.

Maxillae

The maxillae are the basal segments of the palps; they bear a plate at the upper end which usually has a scopula or hairy fringe on the upper edge.

Labium

The labium is situated between the maxillae at the lower end, and is actually the bottom lip of a spider.

Sternum

The sternum is situated behind the labium, and is usually shield-shaped. It is often hollowed out round the margin to receive the bases of the coxa.

Legs

Spiders have four pairs of legs. There are seven segments to each leg and each segment is named. From the carapace they are: coxa, trochanter, femur, patella, tibia, metatarsus and tarsus. They are usually covered with hairs, and sometimes with a variable number of spines and bristles which are called setae. The structure of the legs on some spiders enables them to run sideways; these legs are known as laterigrade legs, and the spiders with them are usually called crab spiders. Normal legs are called prograde legs.

Abdomen

The abdomen or hind section of a spider's body is very variable in size and form. It may either be entirely soft or provided with sigilla or scuta; or entirely hard. On the ventral side are the reproductive and respiratory systems and the spinnerets. Immediately behind the pedicel, the ventral surface is usually chitinised or hard as far as the epigastric furrow, and this area is known as the epigastrium. Centrally positioned and above the epigastric furrow is the epigynum. If present, this is the genital organ of a female spider; it is lacking, however, in mygalomorph spiders. The epigynum is chitinised and often very complex in structure; it is of extreme taxonomic importance. The lung books or lung covers of the first pair of lungs are to be found above the epigastric furrow, and on either side of the epigastrium. The lung openings, at either end of the epigastric furrow, are called lung slits. Most spiders have only one pair of lungs, but in the mygalomorphs a second pair is found below each end of the epigastric furrow. The spiders with one pair of lungs usually have extra respiratory organs, called tracheae, the openings of which are named tracheal spiracles, and are mostly found just above the spinnerets. The spinnerets are situated near the posterior ventral end of the abdomen of most spiders. They are finger-like and are usually arranged in three pairs, known as anterior, median, and posterior spinnerets. The median pair are often very small and completely covered by the anterior and posterior pairs.

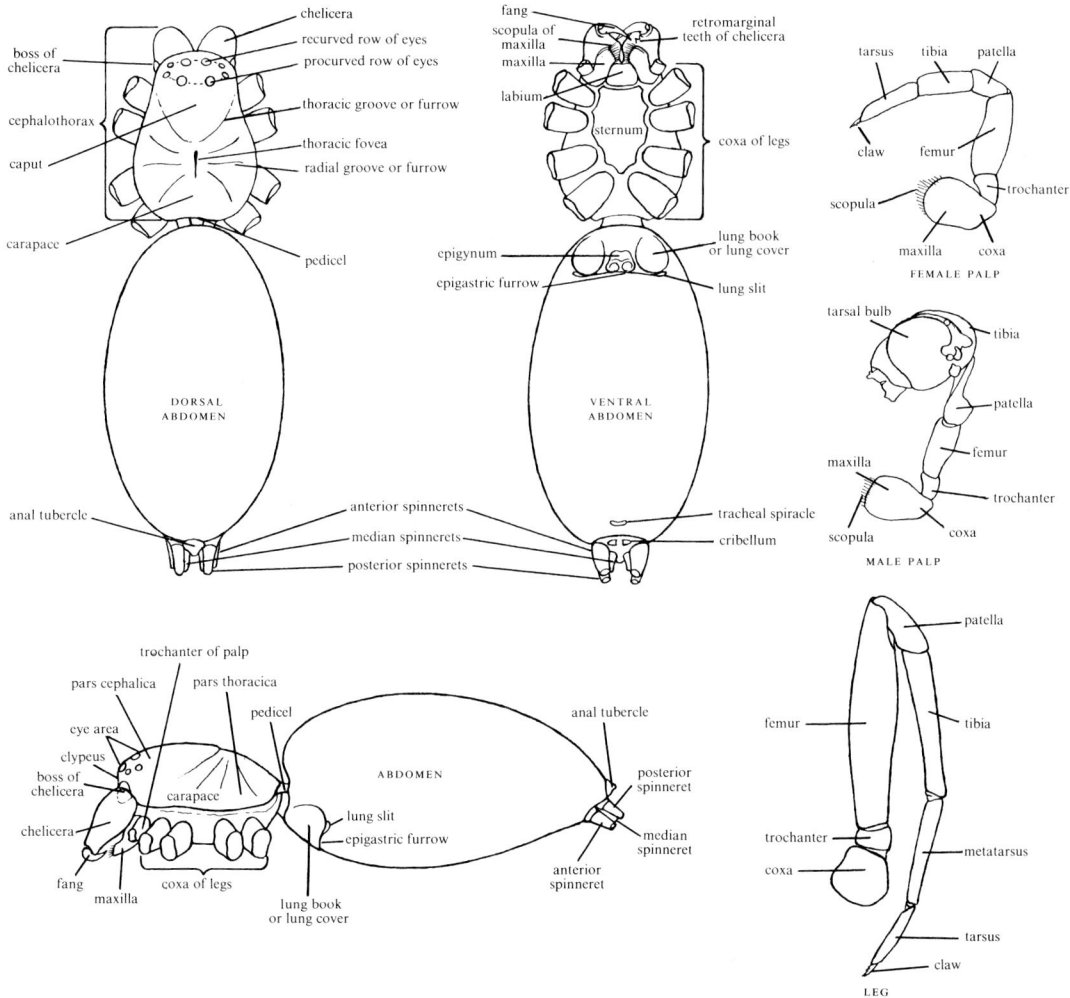

DORSAL ABDOMEN — chelicera, boss of chelicera, recurved row of eyes, procurved row of eyes, cephalothorax, thoracic groove or furrow, caput, thoracic fovea, radial groove or furrow, carapace, pedicel, anal tubercle, anterior spinnerets, median spinnerets, posterior spinnerets

VENTRAL ABDOMEN — fang, scopula of maxilla, maxilla, labium, sternum, retromarginal teeth of chelicera, coxa of legs, epigynum, epigastric furrow, lung book or lung cover, lung slit, tracheal spiracle, cribellum

FEMALE PALP — tarsus, tibia, patella, claw, femur, trochanter, scopula, maxilla, coxa

MALE PALP — tarsal bulb, tibia, patella, femur, trochanter, coxa, maxilla, scopula

Lateral view — trochanter of palp, pars cephalica, pars thoracica, pedicel, eye area, clypeus, boss of chelicera, chelicera, fang, maxilla, coxa of legs, carapace, lung slit, epigastric furrow, lung book or lung cover, ABDOMEN, anal tubercle, posterior spinneret, median spinneret, anterior spinneret

LEG — patella, femur, tibia, trochanter, coxa, metatarsus, tarsus, claw

FIG.1

5

Uses of silk

Although each species has its own habits in the use of silk, all spiders lay eggs and use silk to cover them.

The use of silk in the capture of food is widespread and varied in form, from nets and pitfalls to bolas and triplines, some of the forms having been copied by man.

Some spiders wrap their prey in silk for later use, while others build beautifully-fitted lids to their burrows, and all burrows are silk-lined to some degree.

Many young spiders use silk as a means of dispersal; this is called ballooning. This feat usually takes place a week or so after the young emerge from the egg-sac. The spiderling climbs to a high point, tilts its abdomen upwards in the direction the wind is blowing, and plays out a line or lines of silk. When the pull is great enough, the spiderling releases its hold and is airborne. In this way they are carried great distances.

Several species build a chamber of silk for moulting; others hibernate in a retreat made of silk. Most male spiders build a sperm web on which to secrete the sperm before it is drawn up into the palp.

Copulation

Copulation among spiders is somewhat different to copulation among the insects. Once a male spider reaches maturity, all its energies are directed towards finding a female to mate with, even to the extent of ignoring food. As the palps, or genital organs of the male spider, are not connected to the testes, the palps must first be charged with sperms. To do this, the male builds a small sheet of web, on which it then deposits a drop of seminal fluid. The bulb of the palp is then inserted into the fluid which is sucked up into the bulb. This is called sperm induction.

The male is now ready for copulation, but the method of approaching the female varies with each species. Among the orb-weavers, many males twang the web to woo their intended spouses. If she is not mature or in a co-operative mood, the male will lose his life or some of his limbs when he reaches her. This practice is fairly common among the orb-weavers, but does not apply to many other species.

Males die soon after reaching maturity, and this is probably why the urge to mate is so strong once they are fully grown. Once a male reaches the female to mate he inserts the palps into the epigynum. In some cases the palps are inserted one at a time, in other cases, both together; he then ejects the sperm into the spermathecae, where it is stored to fertilise the eggs as they are laid. The female is able to hold the sperm for considerable periods of time before using it. One female in captivity built an egg-sac nine months after capture; the eggs were fertile, and the young hatched.

Regeneration

The loss of limbs does not appear to inconvenience spiders to any major degree. When a limb is lost, there is no bleeding, and after a short period of time, a thin membrane forms over the stump. After one or two moults, a new limb begins growing from the stump, but never reaches quite the same length as its predecessor.

Poisons

In Australia there are some species of spider which are known to be dangerous to man. There have been at least thirteen deaths from bites of the Sydney Funnel-web Spider *Atrax robustus* (page 14), a few deaths of children from bites of the Red-back Spider *Latrodectus hasselti,* (page 68). Bad bites have been recorded against the Tree Funnel-web Spider *Atrax formidabilis* (page 14), and several cases of severe reaction from bites of the Black House Spider *Ixeuticus robustus* (page 22). Others listed as giving painful or severe bites are: the White-tailed Spider *Lampona cylindrata* (page 40), *Dysdera crocata* (page 16), and the Bird-eating Spider *Selenocosmia crassipes* (page 10). This is a relatively small number of dangerous species in a spider population of over 1,500 known Australian species.

Treatment of Spider Bite

The recommended treatment for a Funnel-web Spider bite is the same as for snake bite. Firm pressure using a crepe bandage or pantyhose should be applied over the bitten area and as much of the limb as possible. A splint should be used to keep the bitten area still. The bandage should be as firm as one would apply to a sprained ankle. Arterial tourniquets are not recommended for any type of bite or sting in Australia.

No special first aid is required for bites by other spiders including the Red-back Spider. A mixture of ice and water in a plastic bag may give some relief of pain.

If the spider can be collected in a jar, take it with the patient for positive identification. Antivenom is available for the bite of the Red-back Spider or a Funnel-web Spider.

Collecting and Preserving

Spiders may be collected by placing a jar under the specimen (if in a web), and bringing the lid down from above. If the specimen is on the ground, it may be encouraged into the jar with a twig—do not handle live spiders. To preserve specimens, they should be kept in ethyl alcohol, and a paper tag with date, place, and collector's name written in lead pencil attached. Dried specimens are useless.

ACKNOWLEDGMENTS

TO MY FRIEND and fellow student Dr John Child I would like to offer many thanks for his encouragement and interest in my work on our spider fauna, and for his many generous gifts of books and equipment, which enabled me to carry on this work.

For their co-operation in processing, and the prompt return of my films, I am greatly indebted to Agfa-Gevaert Ltd. All specimens had to be kept alive until the film results were known. The photographs throughout this book were made exclusively on Agfacolour CT18 reversal film.

No amount of thanks would compensate my good wife for the inconveniences caused by jars of live specimens all over the house, or for the hours spent by her and my daughter Vicki, capturing insects to feed those specimens. To them I offer my humble thanks for all their tolerance shown over the years.

To my good friend Austin Speechley I am indebted for the many interesting, unusual, and new species he has collected for me, and for the photograph he took of me at work.

To Professor V. V. Hickman for his assistance and willingness to impart to me his vast knowledge of our spiders, I offer special thanks.

Special thanks are also due to Mr C. E. Chadwick for the provision of literature and encouragement, and for the many specimens he has collected for me over the years.

To Clyde Coleman of Edmonton, North Queensland I am deeply grateful for many rare and wonderful specimens, together with field notes, and for his continual help and encouragement.

To Ken Farrar, Dallas Doolan, John Cann, Humphrey Osburne, Miss Megan Tilly, and my host of other friends who have collected live specimens for me, and assisted me by supplying transport, I say thanks, once again.

Publisher's note: The family of the late Ramon Mascord and the publisher are grateful to Struan K. Sutherland MD, FRCPA, FRACP, Commonwealth Serum Laboratories, for his assistance in up-dating the Poisons and Treatment of Spider Bite sections in this edition.

GLOSSARY

Abdomen: The second, or posterior, of the two major sections in the body of a spider; the opisthosoma.

ALE: Anterior lateral eye or eyes.

AME: Anterior median eye or eyes.

Anterior spinnerets: The pair nearest the cephalothorax, when looking at the ventral surface of a spider.

Apophysis: A process (heavier than a spine) arising from the male palp, or on the legs.

Book lungs: Respiratory organs, located on the ventral surface of the abdomen, one pair above the epigastric furrow. If present (as in mygalomorph spiders), a second pair are below the epigastric furrow.

Bristle: A hair-like appendage, heavier than a hair and more slender than a spine.

Bulb: The tarsus of the male palp is generally referred to as the genital bulb.

Calamistrum: One or two rows of curved bristles on the fourth metatarsi of the cribellate spiders.

Caput: Head section of the cephalothorax.

Carapace: The hard dorsal covering of the cephalothorax.

Cephalothorax: The first, or anterior, of the two major sections in the body of a spider.

Clypeus: The space between the anterior edge of the carapace and the anterior eyes.

Coxa: That segment of the palps or legs which is nearest the body.

Cribellate: A spider possessing a calamistrum and cribellum.

Cribellum: A plate-like spinning organ, situated in front of the spinnerets of certain spiders, used for producing hackled web.

Diaxial: A term used when the chelicerae project downwards, with the fangs so articulated as to be movable in a transverse plane.

Dorsum: The upper side of the body, particularly of the abdomen.

Endite: A plate on the end of the coxa of the palp, usually called maxilla, or as a pair, maxillae.

Epigastric furrow: A transverse furrow on the ventral surface of the abdomen.

Epigynum: A chitinised structure covering the genital aperture in many female spiders, with openings through which the sperm of the male is passed into the spermathecae.

Fang groove: A groove or furrow at the distal end of the chelicerae, in which the fang fits when not in use.

Fang: The distal, piercing, segment of the chelicerae, through which the poison flows.

Femur: The third segment of the palp and legs, counting from the body.

Folium: A leaf-like pattern on the dorsum of many spiders.

Fovea: A small groove or pit in the centre of the carapace.

Geniculate: Bent like a knee.

Heterogeneous: Unlike; as when some eyes are of dark colour and some of light colour.

Holotype: The single specimen selected by the original author as the type on which a species is based, or the only specimen known at the time of description.

Homogeneous: Alike; as when all eyes are the same colour.

Labium: A conical or flat structure between the maxillae, and above the sternum, on the ventral surface of the cephalothorax.

Lateral eyes: Those eyes which are at the end of the row in which they lie, or the outside eyes.

Laterigrade: A sideways type of locomotion, as in the crab spiders, also used to describe the legs of these spiders.

Lung slits: The external openings to the lungs.

Maxilla: Same as endite, and more frequently used.

Median eyes: The two intermediate eyes of each row.

Median ocular area: The space bordered by the four median eyes.

Median spinnerets: The centre pair which are small and often hidden by other spinnerets.

Metatarsus: The sixth segment of the leg, counting from the body.

MOA: Median ocular area.

Ocellus: A simple eye, as opposed to compound eyes.

Ocular area: That part of the carapace over which the eyes are distributed.

Ocular tubercle: A hump on which one or more eyes are borne.

Palps: The second appendages of the cephalothorax, posterior to the chelicerae, anterior to the legs.

Paratype: A specimen, other than the holotype, upon which an original specific description is based.

Paraxial: When the chelicerae project forward horizontally, and the fang is articulated in a plane more or less parallel to the median plane of the body.

Patella: The fourth segment of leg or palp, counting from the body.

Pectinate: Set with teeth in a row, as in a comb.

Pedicel: The narrow tube connecting the cephalothorax to the abdomen.

Pedipalp: Same as palp.

PLE: Posterior lateral eye or eyes.

PME: Posterior median eye or eyes.

Posterior lateral eyes: The eyes at the end of the posterior row.

Posterior median eyes: The two intermediate eyes of the second row.

Posterior spinnerets: The hind pair when looking at the ventral surface of a spider.

Procurved: Curved forward.

Prograde: Locomotion in a forward direction; the type of legs adapted for such locomotion.

Rastellum: A group of short, stout spines on the apical angle of the basal joint of chelicerae—used for digging.

Rebordered: With a thickened edge.

Recurved: Curved backward.

Scopula: A brush of close-set hairs.

Scuta: Sclerotised plates on the abdomen of some spiders.

Sigilla: Impressed oval or round depressions, marking the attachment of muscles, sometimes present on sternum or abdomen.

Spermathecae: The seminal receptacles in the epigynum.

Spine: A cuticular appendage, considerably heavier than a bristle.

Spinnerets: The finger-like spinning tubes; situated near or at the posterior end of the abdomen.

Spiracle: The opening of the tracheal tube on the ventral surface of the abdomen.

Stabilimentum: A band of dense silk in a web.

Sternum: The ventral plate below the cephalothorax, surrounded by the coxae and below the labium.

Tarsus: The distal segment of the leg or palp.

Tibia: The fifth segment of the leg or palp, counting from the body.

Trichobothria: Very fine sensory hairs, set in sockets on leg or palp.

Trochanter: The second segment of the leg, counting from the body.

MYGALOMORPH SPIDERS

THIS GROUP OF SPIDERS is the most primitive in Australia. They are commonly called Trap-door or Funnel-web spiders, and most of them are terrestrial burrowers. The burrows are varied in form and depth, and may or may not have a lid, all are silk-lined to some degree. The males of this group usually mate in the burrows, and die soon after mating takes place. The females live for many years, and may mate in subsequent years. Mygalomorph spiders may be identified by the par-axial chelicerae, and the presence of four lung books or lung covers—see fig. 2. These spiders are usually of nocturnal habits. The males are vagrants, and will readily attack anything which provokes them, irrespective of size. The females live in the burrows, where they rear the brood. The egg-sac is suspended in the burrow, and after the eggs hatch, the young remain in the burrow with the female for several months. The young disperse during damp weather, when the ground is soft, and dig their own tiny burrows within hours.

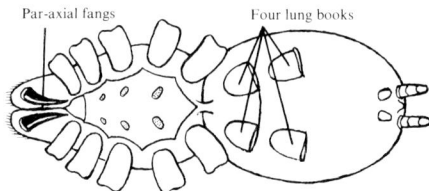

Par-axial fangs   Four lung books

FIG.2

Ventral surface of mygalomorph spider showing four lung books or lung covers, and par-axial chelicerae.

To attack, these spiders raise the front half of their bodies and the front legs off the ground, then strike forwards and downwards. As the spider strikes, it grips the victim with its front legs, and sinks the fangs simultaneously. All mygalomorph spiders should be treated with caution, for some have highly toxic venom, and all can inflict a deep and painful wound, as the fangs are long and strong.

FAMILY THERAPHOSIDAE

Bird-eating Spider *Selenocosmia crassipes*

A veritable giant, the body of this spider reaches a length of 55mm. This species is considered a tropical spider, and is fairly common and wide-spread in Queensland. The male is slightly smaller and slimmer than the female, though still a large and powerful spider. The female pictured killed and ate a half-grown tree frog (*Hyla caerulea*) in six hours. All that remained of the frog after that time was a ball of debris 2cm in diameter, which con-tained bones and skin in a mushy state. When one considers the fact that spiders have no teeth, and mygalomorph spiders rely on digestive fluids to dissolve their food, this feat is remarkable. The fangs of this species may be up to 8.5mm in length, truly formidable weapons. Body length: male up to 40mm, female up to 55mm. Colour: various shades of dusty brown. Identification: by first pair of legs, which are longer and stouter than the fourth pair, with long hairs. Egg-sac: 35mm x 30mm, oval in shape, thicker in the centre, of very white, tough silk. Eggs: 2mm in diameter, translucent, a rich yellow in colour, 48 in number. Burrow: up to 60cm deep, sinuous, with a silken sheet spread from the entrance to entangle prey. Food: small birds (allegedly), frogs, and large insects. This is a nocturnal species. Specimens: No. 1, from Cairns, North Queensland. No. 2, from Tully, North Queensland.

Plate 1
1. *Selenocosmia crassipes* (female) leaving burrow
2. *Selenocosmia crassipes* (male) with a half-grown Green Tree-frog, *Hyla caerulea*

1

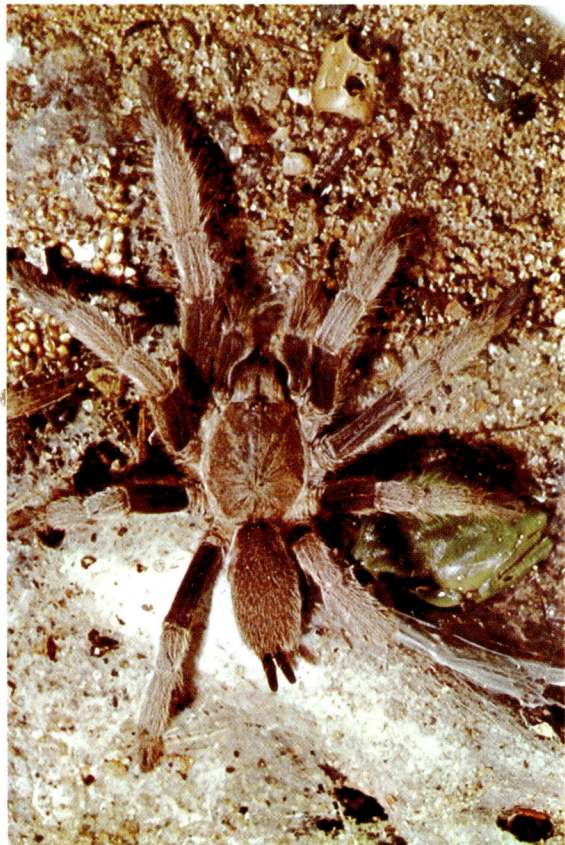

2

FAMILY CTENIZIDAE

Tube Spider *Undescribed species*
This spider inhabits rain-forest country. It is unique among the Trap-door spiders, as it builds a long tube extension above its burrow. The tube extends above the ground for 15–20cm, and is fastened to a rock, tree or fern; it then remains unattached as far as the burrow entrance, to which the other end is fastened. The tube is camouflaged to match whatever it is fastened to at the top, be it tree, fern or rock—even lichens are attached to the tube if present. The burrow continues from the bottom of the tube into the ground for about 10cm, and is silk-lined to this point. Then there is a break in the silk lining for about 2cm, from where it continues for another 20cm, which is all silk-lined, the last 6–7cm being of hard, papery silk. Should the tube be pulled out of the ground, it breaks at the unlined point, thus leaving the spider safe in the lower half of the burrow. Body length: male 17mm, female 27mm. Colour: female as in photograph, male a little darker. Identification: by tube attached to top of burrow. Egg-sac: of rectangular shape, 24mm x 15mm, of white silk, suspended in burrow of female. Eggs: a rich golden-yellow in colour, 50 in number, non-glutinous. Burrow: straight or slightly inclined, no brood shaft present. Dimorphism: male smaller in body, and longer in legs than female. Food: moths, beetles, and other insects, all captured at the mouth of the tube. Specimen: No. 3, from Minnamurra Falls, Kiama, New South Wales.

Brown Trap-door Spider *Dyarcyops fuscipes*
This spider is sometimes referred to as the Sydney Trap-door, though it builds no door to its burrow. It is common in Sydney suburbs, its range extending westwards as far as the mountains. The burrow may be found on level ground, or in banks and slopes. Sometimes the mouth of the burrow extends about one inch above ground level. This species is not known to be dangerous to man. Body length: male 17–19mm, female 25mm. Colour: as in photograph, though sometimes darker on the abdomen. Identification: by photograph and lack of lid on burrow. Egg-sac: rectangular, suspended in burrow of female. Eggs: opaque yellow in colour, 2mm in diameter, 35–50 in number, non-glutinous. Burrow: up to 40cm deep, oblique, silk-lined, occasionally with a brood shaft, although when present, the shaft has no door. Young stay in burrow with the female for several months, then disperse to dig their own tiny burrows, usually after rain. Food debris is stored in the bottom of the burrow. Dimorphism: male smaller in body, and longer in legs than female. Food: moths, crickets, beetles, cockroaches and slaters, all captured in the vicinity of the burrow at night. Specimen: No. 5, from Concord, Sydney; No. 6, from Pittwater, Sydney.

Plate 2
3. Tube Spider (female), *Undescribed species*
4. Tubes of spider fastened to a rock
5. Brown Trap-door Spider, *Dyarcyops fuscipes* (male)
6. Burrow of Brown Trap-door Spider

3

4

5

6

Mouse Spider *Missulena insignis*
A widespread species which is found right across the continent, and often mistaken for *Missulena occatoria*. This species is sometimes found wandering during daylight hours, whereas most mygalomorphs are nocturnal. It is most frequently found in open forest country. The burrows of this species have two doors to the entrance, and a "brood chamber" on one side of the main shaft, which also has a door to it. Body length: male 12mm, female 22mm. Colour: male as illustrated, female dark brown to black, with bases of chelicerae and part of caput reddish-brown. Identification: by broad carapace, across which the small eyes are spread, and short, thick legs. Burrow: vertical, oval at top, round at bottom, up to 30cm deep; brood shaft with a vertical door. Dimorphism: male smaller and slimmer than female. Food: native snails and insects. Specimen: No. 7, from Lithgow, New South Wales.

FAMILY DIPLURIDAE

Tree Funnel-web Spider *Atrax formidabilis*
This very large Funnel-web spider is found in northern New South Wales and southern Queensland. Little is known of its habits, though it was described by W. Rainbow in 1914. The burrow is found in hollow and rotted trees, and its entrance is covered by a curtain of dirty web during daylight hours, which is fastened up at night to leave the burrow entrance clear. The burrow consists of a silken tube in a hole in a tree, and may be over 90cm deep. (A smaller unidentified species has been found by the author in the Sydney area.) Body length: male 35mm, female 65mm. Colour: as in illustration. Identification: by photograph. Dimorphism: males smaller and slimmer than females. Food: frogs and longicorn beetles. Speci-

men: No. 8, from Woodenbong, New South Wales.

Sydney Funnel-web Spider *Atrax robustus*
Probably the world's deadliest spider, certainly Australia's, this species has already been responsible for ten deaths in New South Wales. The venom of the male is more toxic than that of the female, and being vagrants, the males are more likely to be encountered. The females seldom venture far from their burrows unless they are disturbed, or driven out by flooding. Once disturbed, these spiders will attack anything, regardless of size, and when attacking, will strike repeatedly. There is no antivenene for the bite of this species, and though attempts have been made to produce one, so far all have failed. The author suggests the same treatment as for snakebite (see introduction). Body length: male up to 25mm, female up to 40mm. Colour: as in photograph. Identification: by photograph, and shiny black legs and cephalothorax. Burrow: a silken tube which usually ends in a burrow up to 30cm deep. The burrow is mostly situated under a log or stone, a crevice in rocks or beside a tree or post—generally in a cool, damp site. Sometimes there is an extended sheet of web to the burrow entrance. Egg-sac: a rectangular, white, silken envelope, suspended in the burrow of the female. Eggs: 1.4mm in diameter, translucent yellow-green in colour, 90–120 in number. Dimorphism: male smaller and slimmer than female, with longer legs. Specimens: No. 9, from Audley, Sydney; No. 10, from Kiama, New South Wales.

Plate 3
7. *Missulena insignis* (male)
8. *Atrax formidabilis* (female)
9. *Atrax robustus* (female) with venom on fangs
10. *Atrax robustus* (female) in striking position

14

7

8

9

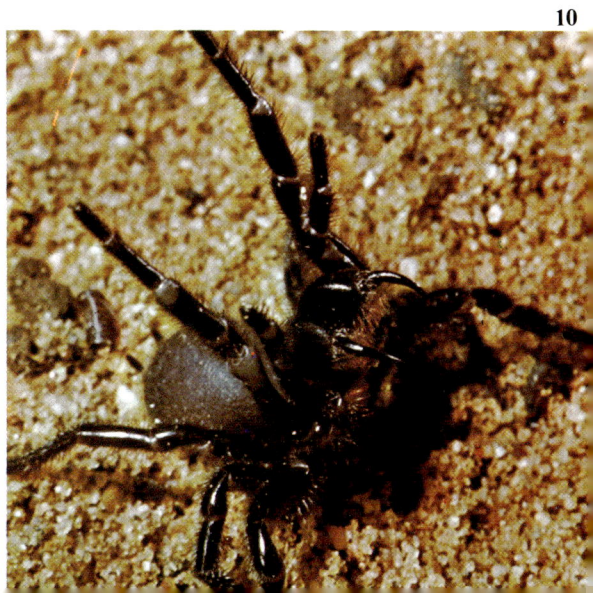

10

No common name *Hexathele hochstetteri*
This species was originally described from New Zealand in 1871 by Ausserer. It is fairly common and widespread in New South Wales, usually found well above sea level. Body length: male 10mm, female 18mm. Colour: light dusty-brown, with lighter chevrons on dorsal surface of abdomen. Identification: by long spinnerets and dorsal pattern. Burrow: a silken tube under stones, logs etc. Egg-sac: unknown to author. Dimorphism: male smaller and slimmer than female. Food: insects. Specimen: No. 11, from Audley, Sydney.

FAMILY PHOLCIDAE

Daddy-long-legs *Pholcus phalangioides*
This is probably the best-known spider in Australia, and is found around most homes. The web is a tangled sheet up to 30cm in diameter. The female carries the egg-sac about in her palps (see photograph No. 12). Body length: male up to 6mm, female 7–8mm. Colour: as in photograph. Identification: by enormously long legs, and body pattern. Egg-sac: a glutinous mass of eggs, held together with a few strands of silk. Dimorphism: male much slimmer and longer in legs than the female. Food: small moths and insects, captured in web. Specimen: No. 12, from Cairns, North Queensland.

FAMILY SCYTODIDAE

Spitting Spider *Scytodes thoracica*
The unique habit of squirting viscous threads from its fangs, and fastening its prey to the strata, makes this spider worthy of mention. There are three endemic species, *S. marmorata*, *S. striatipes* and *S. penicillatus*, *S. thoracica* being introduced. These spiders have only six eyes, whereas most spiders have eight. They are usually found in dry, sheltered places. Body length: male 4mm, female 4.5–5.5mm. Colour: as illustrated. Identification: by the high, domed carapace, six eyes, and slow methodical walk. Egg-sac: a few strands of silk holding the glutinous eggs. Eggs: about 20 in number. Dimorphism: male slightly smaller than female. Food: small insects, mostly silverfish and small moths. Specimen: No. 13, from Mascot, Sydney.

FAMILY DYSDERIDAE

No common name *Dysdera crocata*
This is another introduced species, which was erroneously described as *D. australiensis* by W. Rainbow in 1900. Several severe bites have been recorded from this species. It is usually found in damp sites, under rubbish or stones. Body length: male 10–11mm, female 12–14mm. Colour: as illustrated. Identification: by colour, large fangs, and the presence of six eyes. Egg-sac: a silken retreat, in which the mother seals herself with the eggs until the young are independent. Eggs: 1mm in diameter, rich cream in colour, 25–40 in number. Dimorphism: male slimmer and slightly smaller than female. Food: slaters. Specimen: No. 14, from Botany, Sydney.

Plate 4
11. *Hexathele hochstetteri* (female)
12. *Pholcus phalangioides* (female with egg-sac)
13. *Scytodes thoracica* (female with egg-sac)
14. *Dysdera crocata* (female)

11

12

13

14

FAMILY DINOPIDAE

The members of this remarkable family capture their food by casting a net over it—even moths in flight are sometimes captured. The family contains two genera, *Dinopis* and *Menneus*, the former being the commoner of the two. The genus *Dinopis* is comprised of nine species, the two commonest of which are featured here.

Retiarius Spider *Dinopis bicornis*
A nocturnal spider with a widespread distribution, and common in Sydney suburbs. This species builds a rectangular net after dark and destroys it before daylight, a new net being built each night. The anterior median eyes are of enormous size, and are directed forward, a feature lacking in the genus *Menneus*. During daylight hours, the spider hangs head downward among twigs or dead grass, with its legs stretched out in pairs. This makes it almost impossible to detect, even at close range. The male builds nets until the moult which brings him to maturity, after which the urge to mate is so great that he neglects food and the means of capturing it. After copulation takes place the male dies, which is not uncommon among spiders.

Some time after mating takes place the female builds the egg-sac, fastens one or two leaves around it, then leaves it. The egg-sac is suspended on strong threads about 3cm long, and has a hard waterproof covering. This covering, though tough, is not strong enough to prevent a minute wasp from drilling into it to lay her eggs. The wasps are not parasitic, and emerge from the sac just after the spiderlings have left it. The purpose of this appears to be to save the mother wasp the trouble of building a nest for her eggs. After leaving the egg-sac the spiderlings spin a few strands of fine web, and live in a group for two to three weeks, then disperse by ballooning. Body length: male 15mm, female 20mm. Colour: variable. No. 15 is one of many colour-forms. Identification: by the enormous, black, anterior median eyes, and two light-coloured tubercles, one either side of the abdomen. Egg-sac: spherical, 9mm in diameter, light-brown in colour, black dots sprinkled over the surface, and suspended by one to three strong silken threads, usually with one or more leaves fastened around it. Eggs: 1.6mm in diameter, opaque, cream in colour, 130–150 in number. Web-snare: a rectangular net of crinkly silk, about 3cm x 2cm, which is held by the claws of legs one and two. Dimorphism: male much slimmer and smaller than female, with longer legs. Food: a wide variety of insects including moths. Specimens: Nos 15, 16, and 17 from Botany, Sydney.

Retiarius Spider *Dinopis subrufa*
Though of a different colour to *D. bicornis*, this species has the same habits, and is often found in the same locality. It is found right across the continent, and in Tasmania. Body length: male 14mm, female 23mm. Colour: yellow-brown to grey on the dorsal surface, ventral surface with an orange to red patch running down the centre. Identification: by the huge anterior median eyes, and colour on the ventral surface of abdomen. Egg-sac: similar to, but slightly larger and lighter in colour than the preceding species. Eggs: opaque, pale cream in colour, 2mm in diameter, 120–140 in number. Dimorphism: male smaller, and much slimmer than female. Food: insects of a wide variety. Specimen: from Botany, Sydney.

Plate 5
15. *Dinopis bicornis* (male) after final moult
16. *Dinopis bicornis* (female)
17. Egg-sac of *Dinopis bicornis*
18. *Dinopis subrufa* (female)

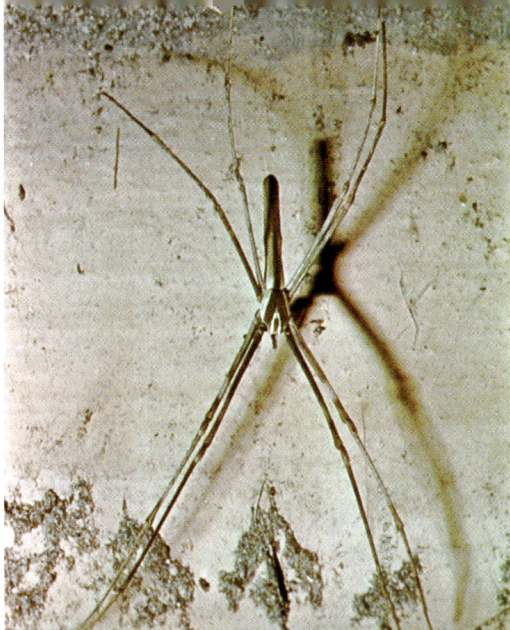

15

16

17

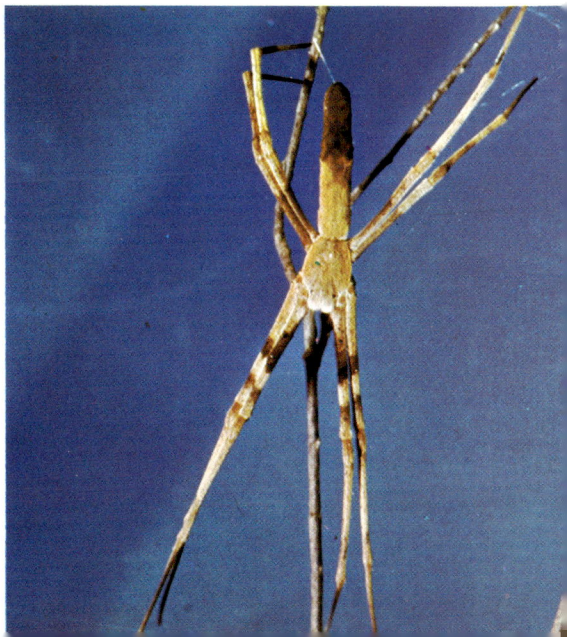

18

Retiarius Spider *Dinopis subrufa*

This photograph shows *Dinopis subrufa* with the net held by the claws of legs one and two. When an insect approaches within range, the spider stretches the net taut and lunges forward and downward, throwing the net over the victim. The more the insect struggles, the more it becomes entangled, and while it is struggling the spider is wrapping the net around it. The victim is then eaten through the net, or wrapping of silk.

Retiarius Spider *Menneus unifasciata*

This species ranges from New South Wales to North Queensland, and though it belongs to the same family as the Dinopids, its habits vary somewhat. The principle variations of habit are: the net is held and cast in a different manner, and the egg-sac is not suspended on threads, but placed in the leaf-litter on the ground. Dinopids usually build their net about 30–40cm from the ground, whereas this genus build theirs two to three times higher, in very tall ferns, or the lower twiggy branches of trees. Dinopids hold their nets by the four corners, *Menneus* hold theirs by the two back corners, and in the centre and on the edge, the front corners are fastened to a thread of silk. Dinopids hold their net flat, *Menneus* fold it in the centre to form a "V". Dinopids are usually found in fairly dry, open country, *Menneus* are found in damp, semi-rain-forest. Dinopids are larger than *Menneus*. Body length: male 7mm, female 9mm. Colour: dusty-brown, a lighter median stripe running the full length of the body on the dorsal surface. Identification: by dorsal stripe, huge anterior median eyes are lacking. Egg-sac: spherical, 4mm in diameter, medium brown in colour, outer case of hard, papery silk, no black dots on outer surface, no suspension threads. Eggs: 0.4mm in diameter, 30 in number, non-glutinous. Dimorphism: male of lighter build, and slightly smaller than female. Web-snare: a rectangular net, which is thrown over prey. Food: small flying insects. Specimens: Nos 20 and 22, from Royal National Park, Audley, Sydney.

Retiarius Spider *Menneus despiciens*

This species is slightly larger than *M. unifasciata*, though of similar habits. Where the former is sometimes found on the edge of semi-rain-forest, this species seems to be confined to darker and thicker regions of the forest. Body length: male 8mm, female 10mm. Colour: variable, depending on the habitat; in very thick areas, the spider is quite dark, as in the illustration. If the foliage is thinner, the spider is usually a dark brown colour. Identification: large anterior median eyes are lacking, distinct flange in centre of abdomen on dorsal surface, smaller than Dinopids. Egg-sac: spherical, 4.5mm in diameter, deep rich brown in colour, outer case of hard, papery silk. The sac is found among leaf-litter on the ground. Eggs: 0.5mm in diameter, deep amber in colour, 47 in number, non-glutinous. Dimorphism: male slightly smaller than female. Web-snare: rectangular net, which is held with the claws of legs one and two, and cast over prey. Food: small flying insects. Specimen: No. 21, from Royal National Park, Audley, Sydney.

Plate 6
19. *Dinopis subrufa* (female) with net
20. *Menneus unifasciata* (male)
21. *Menneus despiciens* (female)
22. *Menneus unifasciata* (female)

19

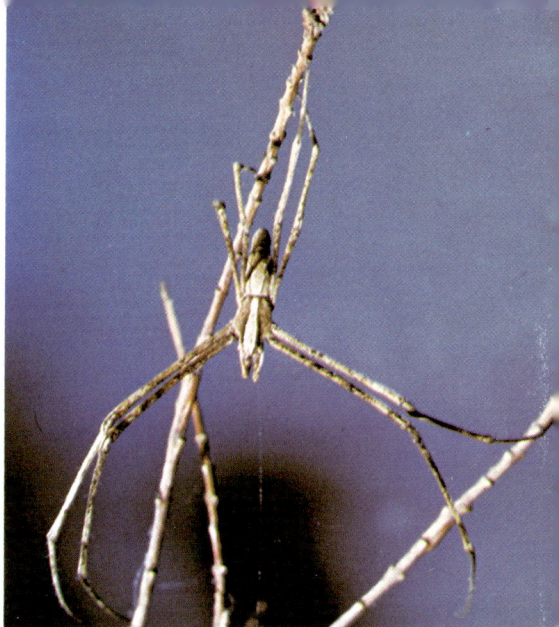

20

21

22

FAMILY DICTYNIDAE

Black House Spider *Ixeuticus robustus*
This species has Australia-wide distribution, and is commonly found around homes. A bite from this spider can be considered dangerous. A friend of the author was bitten on the hand by this species, the symptoms which followed were: severe swelling, localised pain, profuse sweating, shivering and weakness, followed by semi-consciousness. The weakness and sweats continued for several days, then slowly diminished, while the swelling remained for six days before slowly decreasing. The victim suffered for several months with a badly ulcerated hand. Body length: male up to 12mm, female up to 18mm. Colour: as in photograph. Identification: by high blunt carapace, and the web. Egg-sac: plano-convex, of very white silk, placed in the back of the web. Dimorphism: male resembles the female, though somewhat smaller. Food: a wide variety of insects, though moths and flies seem to be preferred. Specimen: No. 23, from Canberra; No. 24, from Botany, Sydney.

No common name *Ixeuticus martius*
Like the previous spider, this species is a cribellate spider, and freshly spun web has a bluish appearance, a characteristic feature of the cribellates. This species is smaller than *I. robustus*, lighter in colour, and its web is usually found in trees and shrubs. Colour: as in photograph, though sometimes a distinct pattern of chevrons is present on the posterior, dorsal surface of the abdomen. Identification: by photograph. Egg-sac: rounded on both sides, of white silk, about 10mm in diameter, suspended at back of web. Eggs: 1mm in diameter, translucent, off-white in colour, 120–180 in number. Dimorphism: male similar to, but slightly smaller than female. Food: a wide variety of insects, including bees. Specimen: No. 25, from Botany, Sydney.

No common name *Ixeuticus candidus*
This species is found right across the continent and in Tasmania. The web is usually found in thick bushes, with a small thimble-like retreat of densely woven, white silk. This retreat also acts as a nursery, for the egg-sac is built within it. The web of this species is often littered with leaves and debris, and in many cases there is a communal web, many families living in a tangle of web, leaves, and debris. Although this species is a cribellate spider, very little zigzag is evident in most webs. Body length: male 7mm, female 9–10mm. Colour: as in photograph. Identification: by photograph. Egg-sac: of very white, fine silk, built on side of the retreat. Food: ants and small insects. Specimen: No. 26, from Royal National Park, Audley, Sydney.

Plate 7
23. *Ixeuticus robustus* (female)
24. Web of *Ixeuticus robustus*
25. *Ixeuticus martius* (female)
26. *Ixeuticus candidus* (female)

23

24

26

25

FAMILY ULOBORIDAE

Humped Spider *Uloborus barbipes*
A small cribellate species, which appears to be restricted to the eastern section of the continent. It builds a small orb web, usually horizontal or obliquely inclined. The spiral threads of the web often have a hackled appearance, particularly towards the centre. The web is mostly in a low position, often fastened to the ground, usually in a sheltered spot, such as under a rock ledge. Most Uloborid spiders sit with the legs stretched straight out when resting in the web; this makes them hard to see, even at close range. Body length: male 3mm, female 4mm. Colour: as in photograph. Identification: by brush of bristles on tibia of leg one. Egg-sac: irregular oval shape, 7mm long, 4mm wide, of dirty-white silk, suspended at the top of the web. The mother guards the sac. Eggs: 0.5mm in diameter, opaque, pink in colour, 42–50 in number, non-glutinous. Dimorphism: male slightly smaller and slimmer than female. Food: small flying insects, including termites when they fly. Specimen: No. 27, from Cooktown, North Queensland.

Humped Spider *Uloborus geniculatus*
A widespread, cosmopolitan species, found wherever settlement has taken place. Usually found in sheltered places, such as in and under houses, in sheds etc. Like the former species, harmless to man. It builds a small orb web, similar to *U. barbipes*. Body length: male 4mm, female 5–6mm. Colour: as illustrated. Identification: by photograph. Egg-sac: about 8mm in diameter, plano-convex, mauve in colour when new, darkening to dirty-brown with age. Dimorphism: male smaller, but similar to female. Food: small flying insects. Specimen: No. 28, from Mascot, Sydney.

FAMILY SALTICIDAE

Jumping Spider *Mopsus penicillatus*
The family name comes from the Latin word *salto*, meaning to dance, and describes this family to perfection. The males perform mating dances to stimulate the females. Many species have metallic colours, particularly those from the tropics. This beautiful species could be considered a tropical spider, as its range is from northern New South Wales to Cape York. Body length: male 12mm, female 15mm. Colour: as illustrated. Identification: by photographs. Egg-sac: disc-shaped, 30mm in diameter, of white silk. Eggs: 1mm in diameter, translucent, rich yellow in colour, 60–80 in number. Dimorphism: male slightly smaller and slimmer than female. These spiders capture their food by jumping and grasping the victim. Food: other spiders and insects. Specimen: Nos 29 and 30, from Cairns, North Queensland.

Plate 8
27. *Uloborus barbipes* (female) with egg-sac
28. *Uloborus geniculatus* (female) with egg-sac
29. *Mopsus penicillatus* (male)
30. *Mopsus penicillatus* (female) with egg-sac

27

28

29

30

Jumping Spider *Sandalodes albobarbatus*
This species was thought to be a northern and central Australian species, but the range is now extended to take in New South Wales. It is an adept jumper, and is usually found under eucalypt bark. The author knows nothing of its breeding habits. Body length: male 8mm, female 10mm. Colour: as illustrated. Identification: by two white spots on either side of abdomen, and a white line round top of abdomen. Egg-sac: unknown to author, as are the eggs. Dimorphism: male slightly smaller, slimmer, and paler than female. Food: insects. Specimen: No. 31, from Springwood, New South Wales.

Ant-mimicking Spider *Myrmarachne striatipes*
Though a jumper, this small spider is better known for its habit of mimicking ants. As is the case with most spiders which mimic ants, the colour of the spider is almost the same as the ant it mimics. When running among ants, it is almost impossible to tell which is which. An ant has three principal divisions to its body, a spider has two. A deep cleft in the cephalothorax of this species, however, gives the impression of a third division. An ant has six legs and antennae, and a spider has eight legs and no antennae. But this species folds the first pair of legs against its body, and uses the tips of them to imitate the antennae of the ant, and runs on six legs. These spiders mix freely with the ants, and feed on them when they get a single ant away from the others. Body length: male 5mm, female 7mm. Colour: as illustrated. Identification: by wedge-shaped chelicerae, and a bronze patch on top of the abdomen. Egg-sac: unknown to the author. Dimorphism: male slightly smaller than female. Food: at least part of their food is comprised of the ants they mimic. Specimen: No. 32, from Wilton, New South Wales.

Jumping Spider *Breda jovialis*
A small but beautiful species, which is found all over Australia and in Tasmania. Like many members of this family, it is usually found under eucalypt bark. Body length: male 6mm, female 9mm. Colour: as illustrated, male brighter. Identification: by unusual colour-pattern, which both sexes have. Egg-sac: a round sac about 9mm in diameter, with a tunnel leading in on opposite sides, of creamy colour. Eggs: 0.9mm in diameter, a rich cream in colour, 25–40 in number. Dimorphism: male smaller, but similar to female. Food: small insects. Specimen: No. 33, from Ryde, Sydney.

Jumping Spider *Cosmophasis micans*
A tropical species, with beautiful metallic markings on the body. This species has been recorded from North Queensland, New Guinea, Malaysia and Pelew Island. The author knows nothing of its habits or breeding, and it was included for its brilliance of colour. Body length: male 6mm, female 7mm. Colour: as illustrated. Identification: by brilliant colour-pattern on the body. Egg-sac and eggs: unknown. Dimorphism: male slightly smaller and much slimmer than female. Food: probably small insects. *Note:* this species was described under the genus *Plexippus* in 1846, and under the genus *Amycus* in 1880, but has now been placed in the genus *Cosmophasis* with a query. Specimen: No. 34, from Cairns, North Queensland.

Plate 9
31. *Sandalodes albobarbatus* (male and female)
32. *Myrmarachne striatipes* (female)
33. *Breda jovialis* (female)
34. *Cosmophasis micans* (male)

31

32

33

34

Gliding Spider *Saitis volans*
This is probably our most beautiful spider, and only the male is known to science. Though a jumping spider, it is better known for its ability to glide. This is achieved per medium of two "flaps", one on either side of the abdomen, which have a long, hairy fringe on the outer edges. When not in use, these flaps fold under the abdomen, where they almost meet in the centre of the ventral surface of the abdomen. To use these flaps the spider jumps, then extends the flaps and holds them rigid so that they act as wings, and the jump ends in a glide. These midgets can cover considerable distances with this jump-glide combination, and though the spider is only 4–5mm in body length, he can cover a distance of up to 17cm. Body length: male 4–5mm, female unknown. Colour: male as illustrated. Identification: by colour and flaps. Egg-sac: unknown. Food: small insects. Specimen: No. 35, from Pittwater, Sydney.

Jumping Spider *Astia hariola*
A small jumping spider which is strikingly marked, this species is found in New South Wales and Queensland. It is usually found under eucalypt bark. The male is the brighter coloured of the sexes. Body length: male 5mm, female 6–7mm. Colour: female as illustrated, male much brighter. Identification: by colour and pattern. Egg-sac: disc-shaped, about 10mm in diameter, of white silk, usually fastened under bark. Eggs: opaque, pale cream in colour, 37–50 in number. Dimorphism: male smaller and slimmer than female. Food: small insects and ants. Specimen: No. 36, from Armidale, New South Wales.

Jumping Spider *Sigytes scutulata*
A small species found in New South Wales and Queensland. Described in 1881, as *Ergane scutulata* by Keyserling, it was changed later to its present name. Nothing is known of its habits. Body length: male 5mm, female 7mm. Colour: as illustrated. Identification: by photograph. Egg-sac and eggs are unknown. Dimorphism: male smaller and slimmer than female. Food: small insects. Specimen: No. 37, from Berry, New South Wales.

Jumping Spider *Holoplatys planissima*
A small, flat jumping spider, with a body adapted for entering cracks and folds in bark. It is usually found under eucalypt bark, or in folds of bark, tiny crevices etc. William Rainbow lists this spider as being a northern and western species, but the author has found several specimens in New South Wales. These specimens were collected over a wide area in this state, so it can now be considered a New South Wales species. Body length: male 6mm, female 8mm. Colour: as illustrated. Identification: by its jerky locomotion, and two parallel indentations running the full length of its abdomen. The male also has a short scute on the dorsal anterior end of its abdomen. Egg-sac and eggs: these have not been recorded. Dimorphism: male smaller and slimmer than female. Food: small insects which inhabit the bark of trees, particularly false scorpions. Specimen: No. 38, from Parramatta, New South Wales.

Plate 10
35. *Saitis volans* (male)
36. *Astia hariola* (female)
37. *Sigytes scutulata* (female)
38. *Holoplatys planissima* (female)

28

35

36

37

38

Jumping Spider *Bavia ludicra*
This species ranges from North Queensland down the east coast to Tasmania. It is quite large in comparison with most jumping spiders, and the male is almost as large as the female, but with much longer legs and a different body pattern. These spiders are usually found under eucalypt bark, or in rolled bark which hangs from many of our eucalypts. Keyserling described a different species as the male in 1882, but this is understandable, as the description was based on a dead specimen sent to Germany. Body length: male 10mm, female 12–13mm. Colour: as in illustrations. Identification: by colour patterns in illustrations. Egg-sac and eggs: unknown to author, though the mating takes place in spring. Food: bark-dwelling insects and spiders. Dimorphism: male with longer legs, but body length almost equal to female. Specimens: No. 39, from East Kurrajong, New South Wales, No. 40, from Gladesville, Sydney.

Jumping Spider *Ocrisiona leucocomis*
Another of the bark-dwelling jumping spiders, which also has a rather flat body. This species is fairly widespread, being found in New South Wales, Queensland, Western Australia, and New Zealand. The eggs are laid in a white silken retreat on the inner surface of eucalypt bark. Body length: male 8mm, female 11mm. Colour: as illustrated. Identification: by flat appearance and body pattern in photograph. Egg-sac: a white, round sac 6mm in diameter, which is built within a silken retreat. Eggs: 1mm in diameter, opaque, pale cream in colour, 25–40 in number, non-glutinous. Dimorphism: male smaller than female. This spider builds no web-snare. Food: bark-inhabiting insects and other small spiders. Specimens: No. 41, female *(left)* and male *(right)*, from North Ryde, Sydney.

Jumping Spider *Plexippus validus*
A widespread species in eastern New South Wales, commonly found under loose eucalypt bark, sometimes under loose wattle bark. This species is rather broader than most species of jumping spiders, and very variable in colour. Males and females are often found under the one piece of bark. Body length: male 8mm, female 8–10mm. Colour: variable, but usually similar to photograph, though sometimes more reddish-brown. Identification: by photograph, and chevrons on posterior end of abdomen. Egg-sac: oval in shape, about 10mm in diameter, of white silk. Eggs: pale amber in colour, 1mm in diameter, 35–50 in number, non-glutinous. Dimorphism: males slightly smaller than females, legs one and two longer than those of the female. Food: bark-dwelling insects, and occasionally other small spiders. (The author has found this species eating *Euryopis splendens* on two occasions.) Specimen: No. 42, from Holsworthy, New South Wales.

Plate 11
39. *Bavia ludicra* (male)
40. *Bavia ludicra* (female)
41. *Ocrisiona leucocomis* (female) *left*, (male) *right*
42. *Plexippus validus* (female)

39

40

41

42

FAMILY SELENOPIDAE

No common name *Selenops australiensis*
This widespread species is the only member of the family found in Australia. Though similar in appearance and habit to the huntsmen spiders (see below) it differs in two respects. This species has six eyes in the front row, with a single eye behind each lateral eye of the front row. Secondly, there is no scopula on the legs, which the huntsmen have. When resting, all legs are turned towards the front, and the body is pressed flat against the surface on which the spider is resting. Body length: male 6–7mm, female 8–9mm. Colour: variable, from light brown to dark brown, legs always annulated. Identification: by illustration. Egg-sac and eggs are unknown to the author. Dimorphism: male slightly smaller, but similar to female. No web-snare is built. Food: a wide range of small insects, which the spider pounces on. Specimens: No. 43, (female) *left,* (male) *right,* from Wyong, New South Wales.

FAMILY SPARASSIDAE

Huntsman Spider *Isopeda immanis*
This is one of the largest huntsmen spiders found in Australia. This species is usually found under the bark of trees, but occasionally it is seen under logs and stones. The distribution of this species appears to be East Australia, from Queensland to Victoria. Body length: male 30mm, female 47mm. Colour: as illustrated. Egg-sac: oval, flat, 25mm long, of very white, papery silk. Eggs: unknown to the author. Dimorphism: male slimmer and smaller than female, with longer legs. Food: large insects, including moths and beetles, which the spider pounces on. Specimen: No. 44, from West Ryde, Sydney.

Huntsman Spider *Delena cancerides*
Another very large species of huntsman which is widespread throughout Australia and Tasmania. Like the previous species, the female guards her egg-sac and her young until they are about half-grown, and resents any interference with them. These two species are not known to be dangerous to man, notwithstanding their large size. Body length: male 21–25mm, female 25–28mm. Colour: as illustrated. Identification: by photograph. Egg-sac: 25–30mm in diameter, of very white silk, fastened to wall of retreat, which is usually under eucalypt bark. Eggs: 1.7mm in diameter, deep yellow in colour, 130–170 in number. Dimorphism: male smaller and slimmer than female. No web-snare is built. Food: a wide range of insects. Specimen: No. 45 (male), from Hartley, New South Wales.

Huntsman Spider *Heteropoda cervina*
This species is a bark-dwelling spider, which was described by L. Koch in 1875 under the name *Sarotes cervinus;* Simon altered the name to its present status in 1880. Despite the fact that this spider has been known for so long, very little is known of its habits. By including it in this book, it is hoped some student will add to the field notes of the species. Body length: male 18mm, female 23mm. Colour: as illustrated. Identification: by photograph. Egg-sac: unknown. Food: a wide range of insects, particularly moths. Specimen: No. 46 (female), from Tully, North Queensland.

Plate 12
43. *Selenops australiensis* (female) *left,* (male) *right*
44. *Isopeda immanis* (male)
45. *Delena cancerides* (male)
46. *Heteropoda cervina* (female)

43

44

45

46

The genus *Olios* contains many species which are almost identical on the dorsal surface and in general appearance. The scientific method of determining a species is to study the genitalia, which requires a microscope and drawings of the genital organs. Most species of this genus differ on the ventral surface of the abdomen, so a photograph of both surfaces has been included. This will make identification easier for the layman. These spiders are usually found on or under the bark of trees, particularly eucalypts, and often the mother is found guarding her large egg-sac, or with young in attendance. The eggs of the different species vary from opaque white to deep yellow or bright green. The colours on the under-surface of the legs are often quite brilliant.

Huntsman Spider *Olios pictus*
This species has a very wide distribution, being found over most of the continent, and is common in New South Wales. Body length: male 13mm, female 18mm. Colour: as illustrated. Identification: by the ventral pattern of the abdomen. Egg-sac: round, flat on top, rounded underneath, of very white, papery silk. The female guards the eggs and young. Eggs: 1.2mm in diameter, deep yellow in colour, 120–150 in number. Dimorphism: male smaller and slimmer than the female, and legs one and two are longer. Food: moths and bark-dwelling insects such as Click beetles and Longicorn beetles. Specimen: No. 47 (male) dorsal, No. 48 (male) ventral, from Waterfall, Sydney.

Huntsman Spider *Olios salacius*
This species appears to be confined to the eastern section of Australia, from New South Wales to Cape York. It is usually found under the bark on trees, or in logs and stumps, and is a nocturnal species, as are most of this genus. Body length: male 16mm, female 20mm. Colour: as in photograph. Identification: by the ventral pattern of the abdomen. The egg-sac and eggs are unknown to the author. Dimorphism: the male is smaller and slimmer, and with longer legs than the female. Food: moths and a wide variety of insects, particularly night-flying species. These are captured when they land on the bark of trees, where the spider usually sits at night. Specimen: No. 49 (female) dorsal, No. 50 (female) ventral, from Cooktown, North Queensland. *Note:* Two common species with a wide distribution are *Olios diana* and *Olios calligaster*. *O. diana* may be identified by the ventral pattern of the abdomen—a black shield-shaped patch below the epigastric furrow, which has two very white spots or bars in the centre. Below the black patch is a smaller patch of bright orange. *O. calligaster* has a black triangular patch on the ventral surface of the abdomen, the white spots or bars in the centre of the patch are lacking, as is the smaller orange patch below it. Two species of *Olios* have been recorded as giving painful and reactive bites to humans. They are *Olios calligaster* and *Olios punctatus*. As these spiders do not readily bite, there could be more species which could give painful bites if provoked.

47

48

49

50

Huntsman Spider *Olios patellatus*

This species is often mistaken for *Olios diana*, but the shield-shaped black patch of *O. diana* is replaced with a smaller T-shaped patch, and the white bars on this species are outside the black patch, not inside. Dr Karsch originally placed this species in the genus *Heteropoda* when he described it in 1875, it has since been changed to the genus *Olios*. It was thought that this species was restricted to Tasmania, and the author has only found it in one area in Australia, which is a hanging swamp some 2,000 feet above sea level. The spiders were living in the foliage of *Banksia serrata*, and were in a retreat made of leaves bound together with silk. Body length: male 18mm, female 21mm. Colour: as illustrated. Identification: by the ventral pattern of abdomen. Egg-sac: round, flat on top, rounded slightly underneath, about 20mm in diameter, of papery, yellowish silk. Eggs: unknown to author. Dimorphism: male similar to female, though slightly smaller. Food: mostly moths. Specimen: No. 51 (female) dorsal, No. 52 (female) ventral, from Barren Grounds Faunal Reserve, between Robertson and Kiama, New South Wales.

Lichen Spider *Pandercetes gracilis*

This remarkable spider adopts the same colour as the lichens growing on the tree trunks in the rainforests of North Queensland. The egg-sac is built on the lichen-covered bark, and is camouflaged to match the bark. Once the egg-sac is built, the mother sits with her legs resting on the sac, and she remains in this position for long periods. Once disturbed, she runs sideways, then "freezes" again. Her camouflage is so good that one has to be almost on top of the spider to detect it. When first hatched, the young climb over, and even sit on the mother, but she ignores them unless they get on her eyes, in which case she brushes them off with leg one. The young hatch and leave the egg-sac in late summer.

Body length: male 8mm, female 13mm. Colour: as illustrated. Identification: by the coloured photograph. Egg-sac: oval in shape, 20mm in length, 15mm wide at its widest point. The outer case is of paper-like silk, mottled to match the surrounds. It is of flocculent silk inside, domed in the centre, and tapering to the edges. Eggs: 1mm in diameter, opaque, pale cream in colour, 112 counted in the sac. Dimorphism: the male is smaller in the body than the female, with longer legs. Food: moths and other bark-dwelling insects. Specimens: Nos 53 and 54 (both females) from Cairns, North Queensland.

Plate 14
51. *Olios patellatus* (female) dorsal
52. *Olios patellatus* (female) ventral
53. *Pandercetes gracilis* (female) with egg-sac
54. *Pandercetes gracilis* (female) with young

51

52

53

54

Huntsman Spider *Pediana regina*
This species was originally described by L. Koch in 1875 as *Heteropoda regina*. In 1880, Simon found that it did not conform with the key to the genus *Heteropoda*, so he erected the genus *Pediana*, and made this species the type. Four species of the genus are found in Australia; one from South Australia, two from West Australia, and the species illustrated, from Queensland. These spiders are rather shorter in the legs than most huntsmen spiders, and are usually found in or on old logs and tree stumps, or under bark at the base of trees. Body length: male 19mm, female 25mm. Colour: as illustrated. Identification: by dorsal and ventral colour patterns, as illustrated. Egg-sac and eggs; unknown to the author. Dimorphism: male smaller, more slender, and slightly longer in the legs than the female. Food: bark-dwelling insects and other spiders. Specimen: No. 55 (dorsal), and No. 56 (ventral), from Mirriam Vale, Queensland.

FAMILY CLUBIONIDAE

No common name *Miturga lineata*
The genus *Miturga* contains the largest members of this family, some species reaching a body length of 20mm. This is a widespread species, having been recorded from New South Wales, Victoria and Central Australia. A large retreat of dense, very white silk is built in grass, low tussocks, under bark on the ground, or even on bushes, but always close to the ground. The retreat is usually built like a bag, with several openings, and may be up to 15cm in length. This retreat is also used as a nursery, as the egg-sac is built within it, and fastened to the side of the silken wall. Several egg-sacs are sometimes found in one retreat. When disturbed, the spider quickly runs out of one of the openings, and hides in the grass. Owing to the colour pattern of its body, it is very difficult to detect, particularly when the grass is dead.

Body length: male 11mm, female 20mm. Colour: variable, from grey to brown. Identification: by photograph, and the presence of four white stripes on the ventral surface of the abdomen. These stripes run from the epigastric furrow to the spinnerets. Egg-sac: flattened at the edges, raised in the centre, round to oval in shape, up to 1.5cm in diameter. Eggs: 1mm in diameter, an opaque off-white colour, up to 100 in number. Dimorphism: males smaller and slimmer than females. Food: a wide variety of insects, captured at night. Specimen: No. 57, from Malabar, Sydney.

No common name *Miturga gilva*
This appears to be an eastern species, being found in Queensland, New South Wales, and Victoria. As with the previous species, a silken retreat is built close to the ground, though the silk is not so white as that of *M. lineata*. Body length: male 10mm, female 18mm. Colour: as illustrated. Identification: by photograph. Egg-sac: round, raised in the centre, sloping to the edges, 1cm in diameter. Eggs: 1mm in diameter, very pale cream in colour, 80–100 in number. Dimorphism: male more slender and longer in legs than female. Food: ground-dwelling insects. Specimen: No. 58, from Gloucester, New South Wales.

Plate 15
55. *Pediana regina* (female) dorsal
56. *Pediana regina* (female) ventral
57. *Miturga lineata* (female)
58. *Miturga gilva* (male)

55

56

57

58

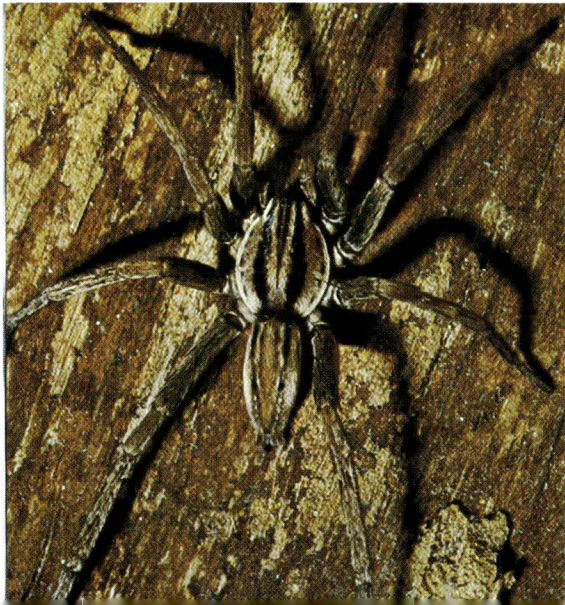

FAMILY DRASSIDAE

White-tailed Spider *Lampona cylindrata*
Many authors include these spiders in the family Gnaphosidae. But the modern trend is towards Drassidae. This species is considered dangerous to man, and though no deaths have been recorded against it, there are several cases of severe illness from its bite. This spider is usually found under stones or the bark of trees, though it frequently inhabits bathrooms of homes. It seems to prefer cool places, and often builds a tubular retreat of silk, though many are found wandering. It is found right across Australia, and in Tasmania and New Zealand. Body length: male 12mm, female 17mm. Colour: as illustrated, though the white marks on the abdomen of the female get paler with age. Identification: by photograph. Egg-sac: circular, 10mm in diameter, of fine, white silk. Eggs: 1.2mm in diameter, pink in colour, non-glutinous, up to 90 in number. Dimorphism: male much slimmer and smaller than female. Food: mostly other spiders. Specimens: No. 59 (male), from Malabar, Sydney; No. 60 (female), from Gawler, South Australia.

No common name *Hemicloea plumea*
The *Hemicloeas* are all flat spiders, and are usually found under stones and bark. The female is often found guarding the egg-sacs; sitting with her front legs resting on the sacs. This species is restricted to New South Wales and Queensland, and does not appear to be plentiful in any area. Body length: male unknown, female 15mm. Colour: as illustrated. Identification: by flat body, and photograph. Egg-sac: round, of dirty-white silk, about 10mm in diameter. Eggs: unknown to the author. Dimorphism: unknown. Food: small cockroaches seem to be preferred. A nocturnal species. Specimen: No. 61, from Royal National Park, Audley, Sydney.

No common name *Hemicloea major*
This large species appears to be confined to New South Wales, and is fairly common in the sandstone ridges around Sydney. This spider was described by L. Koch in 1875, from a specimen collected in Sydney, and sent to Germany. With the clearing of land in the Sydney area, this species is fast disappearing. In many areas where this spider was plentiful three years ago (1966), it has completely vanished. Bush fires also contribute in the destruction of many species of ground spiders. Body length: male 18mm, female 28mm. Colour: as illustrated. Identification: by its large size, flat body, and the photograph. Egg-sac: circular, 20–28mm in diameter, dirty-white to dusty-brown in colour, with a granulated surface. Three or four sacs are usually found, one often built partly over another. Eggs: 1.2mm in diameter, opaque, a very pale cream in colour, up to 80 in each sac. Food: a wide variety of insects and other spiders. Specimen: No. 62, from Canberra.

Plate 16

59

60

61

62

No common name *Rebilus lugubris*

This genus is very similar in habit and form to *Hemicloea*, and is also placed in the family Gnaphosidae by some authors. The principal difference between the genera is the spinnerets. *Hemicloea* have six spinnerets, *Rebilus* have four spinnerets and two curved plates between them, each plate having a double row of openings. Body length: male 12mm, female 16mm. Colour: from very dark brown to black. Identification: by spinnerets and photograph. Egg-sac: circular, 20mm in diameter, of very white, smooth silk, no granulations on the surface. Eggs: 1.2mm in diameter, opaque, pale cream in colour, non-glutinous, 40–50 in number. Dimorphism: male smaller in the body, but with much longer legs than the female. Food: bark and ground-dwelling insects. Specimen: No. 63 (female), from Minnamurra Falls Reserve, Kiama, New South Wales.

FAMILY MIMETIDAE

No common name *Mimetus maculosus*

The members of this family live on other spiders, and this species will readily attack and eat Red-back spiders, or any other long-legged species about its own size. The poison from these spiders does not appear to have any effect, unless the victim is bitten on the leg, then it is fast acting. Body length: male 5.2mm, female 8.1mm. Colour: as illustrated, though the mottling varies. Identification: by photograph and legs one and two, which have a series of large spines on the prolateral surface, with a row of curved, smaller spines between the large ones. Egg-sac: tear-shaped, 10mm long, 5mm wide at the widest point, of fine, lacey silk, eggs visible in the centre. Eggs: 1.1mm in diameter, rich yellow in colour, 50–70 in number. Dimorphism: male

smaller and slimmer than female. Specimen: No. 65, from Royal National Park, Audley, Sydney.

No common name *Mimetus audax*

This species is of similar habits to *M. maculosus*, though it is slightly smaller and of a different colour. As with the previous species, the web consists of a few single strands of silk. Body length: male 5mm, female 6mm. Colour: as illustrated: the male lacks the dark patch on abdomen, though it is speckled with black. Identification: by photograph and spines on legs one and two, as in previous species. Egg-sac: tear-shaped, of bright orange silk, 7mm long, 3.2mm wide at the widest point. Eggs: bright orange in colour, 1mm in diameter, 40–50 in number. Dimorphism: male slightly smaller than female. Food: other spiders. *Note:* The male of this species is undescribed. Specimen: No. 65 (female), from Royal National Park, Audley, Sydney.

No common name *Mimetus species*

This undescribed species was only found through patience and perseverance by a friend. He found the egg-sac among thousands of plant pots five years ago, and though he searched regularly, the spider, a female, was only recently captured. Body length: female 7mm. Colour: as illustrated. Identification: by photograph. Egg-sac: circular, 5mm in diameter, of fine, gauze-like white silk, eggs plainly visible in centre. Eggs: deep yellow, 1mm in diameter, 52 in number. Food: other spiders. Specimen: No. 66 (female), from Botany, Sydney.

Plate 17
63. *Rebilus lugubris* (female) with egg-sac
64. *Mimetus maculosus* (female) with egg-sac
65. *Mimetus audax* (female) with egg-sac
66. *Mimetus species* (female)

63

64

65

66

FAMILY THOMISIDAE

Crab Spider *Tmarus marmoreus*
The family Thomisidae do not build web-snares of any kind; they capture their food by grasping it with their front legs. It is a very large family, comprised mostly of small spiders which can run sideways as well as forward. The genus *Tmarus* build small retreats by folding the tip of a leaf or a blade of grass, and binding it with silk to form the retreat. They are sometimes found at night hanging from a single strand of silk. Body length: male 4mm, female 5.3mm. Colour: as in photograph. Identification: by high caput, and illustration. Egg-sac: a small disc-shaped sac, fastened to lid of retreat. Eggs: 0.7mm in diameter, translucent, off-white colour, non-glutinous, 25–40 in number. Dimorphism: male noticeably slimmer than female, but legs much longer. Food: small insects. Specimen: No. 67 (female), from Pittwater, Sydney.

Crab Spider *Tmarus cineraceus*
This species is of similar habit to the previous one, and is fairly common in the Sydney area, though hard to find because of its coloration, and its habit of sitting still on a dead twig. Body length: male 3.5mm, female 5mm. Identification: by photograph and high caput. Egg-sac: similar to previous species, though slightly smaller in size. Eggs: 0.6mm in diameter, an opaque, cream colour, about 30 in number. Dimorphism: male slimmer, but longer in legs than the female. Food: small insects. Specimen: No. 68 (female), from Royal National Park, Audley, Sydney.

Crab Spider *Bomis larvata*
This species is probably the smallest of the family, being only 2mm long in the body of an adult female. The specimen illustrated was collected from the flowers of *Senecio vagus*, a native plant which has a yellow flower. The retreat of this midget was a folded serration on the edge of the leaf. Body length: male 1.4mm, female 2mm. Colour: as in photograph. Identification: by size and illustration. Egg-sac: in retreat, round, 2mm in diameter, of fine, white silk. Eggs: 0.5mm in diameter, translucent, off-white colour, 6 in number, glutinous. Dimorphism: male similar to, but smaller than female. Food: unknown. Specimen: No. 69 (female), from Royal National Park, Audley, Sydney.

Crab Spider *Cymbacha festiva*
These spiders also build a retreat, mostly using the tip of a leaf and folding it into a small bell tent, though sometimes they fold a blade of grass. They are often found overhanging creeks or rivers, usually in shady areas. Body length: male 3.5mm, female 4mm. Colour: as illustrated. Identification: by photograph. Egg-sac: in retreat, 3.6mm in diameter, of fine, white silk, round. Eggs: 0.7mm in diameter, opaque, off-white in colour, 25–40 in number. Dimorphism: male slightly smaller, but similar to female. Food: small insects. Specimen: No. 70 (female), from Springwood, New South Wales.

Plate 18
67. *Tmarus marmoreus* (female) with sac
68. *Tmarus cineraceus* (female)
69. *Bomis larvata* (female) with sac
70. *Cymbacha festiva* (female) with sac

67

68

69

70

Crab Spider *Cymbacha setosa*
A small species which builds a retreat by folding the tip of a leaf, or a blade of grass. The retreat later acts as a nursery. L. Koch described this species in 1874, from a specimen collected at Rockhampton, Queensland, and sent to Germany. Though not common in New South Wales, it has been collected as far south as Sydney. Body length: male 3mm, female 3.5mm. Identification: by the tiny spines which cover the legs. Egg-sac: the sac is fastened inside the retreat, circular in shape, of very white silk, 3.7mm in diameter. Eggs: 0.6mm in diameter, opaque, very pale cream in colour, numbering 19 in the sac examined. Dimorphism: male slightly smaller than female. Food: very small insects. Specimen: No. 71 (female), from Royal National Park, Audley, Sydney.

Crab Spider *Cymbacha ocellata*
This species is probably the best-known of the genus, because of the brighter body pattern. Body length: male 4.3mm, female 6–7mm. Colour: as illustrated. Identification: by the dorsal pattern of the abdomen. Egg-sac: fastened to side of retreat, 3.5mm in diameter, of tough, very white silk. Eggs: 0.8mm in diameter, of pale cream colour, 12 in number. Dimorphism: male smaller than female. Food: small insects. Specimen: No. 72 (female), from Mount Druitt, New South Wales.

Crab Spider *Cymbacha species*
This spider has been parasitised by an insect, and the small white objects seen on it are the larvae of the insect. When collected, the spider was quite robust, and the larvae were tiny. Seven days later, the spider had withered considerably, and the larvae had grown enormously. Normally, the spider would live long enough to bring the larvae to maturity, as only one or two eggs are placed on the victim. In this case, the spider was probably parasitised by more than one insect, and died ten days after capture, so the effort was wasted. The spider was identified by the genus only, and was too withered for any study after death, so no description is available. Body length: female 7.4mm. Specimen: No. 73 (female), from Royal National Park, Audley, Sydney.

Crab Spider *Tharpyna munda*
These tiny spiders inhabit the bark of eucalypts, and being nocturnal, are seldom seen by the public. This species has been found by the author only on black bark. Body length: male 4.5mm, female 5mm. Identification: by dorsal pattern on the abdomen. Egg-sac: oval in shape, made of dirty-white silk, covered with debris, usually built on the under-surface of bark. Eggs: unknown to the author. Dimorphism: male more slender in the body, and with longer legs than the female. Food: small, bark-dwelling insects. Specimen: No. 74 (male), from Ku-ring-gai Chase National Park, Sydney.

Plate 19
71. *Cymbacha setosa* (female) with sac
72. *Cymbacha ocellata* (female)
73. *Cymbacha species* (female)
74. *Tharpyna munda* (male)

71

72

73

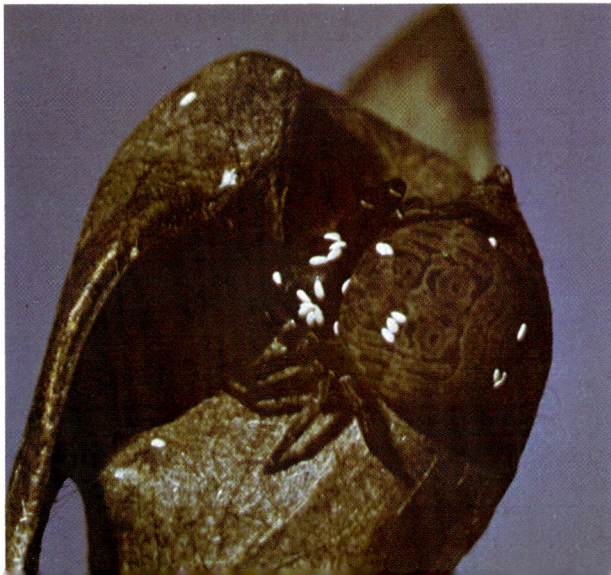

74

Crab Spider *Tharpyna campestrata*

This small but beautiful species was described by L. Koch in 1874, from specimens sent to him in Germany, collected at Cape York, North Queensland. It appears to be common west of the Dividing Range in New South Wales, and the author found it in large numbers at Glen Davis and surrounding districts. It frequents the bark of eucalypts, but being a nocturnal species, is seldom seen during daylight hours unless loose bark is lifted. Body length: male 7mm, female 9mm. Colour: variable, from shades of brown to almost purple. Identification: by dorsal pattern on the abdomen. Egg-sac: oval in shape, 10mm long, 6mm wide at its widest point. Eggs: 0.8mm in diameter, cream in colour, non-glutinous, 30–40 in number. Dimorphism: male identical to, though smaller than female. Food: leaf hoppers and other small bark-dwelling insects. Specimens: Nos 75 and 76 (male and female), from Glen Davis, New South Wales.

Crab Spider *Thomisus spectabilis*

This is the only species of this genus recorded from Australia. When L. Koch described it in 1867, he placed it in the genus *Xysticus*, and named it *X. pustulosus*. In 1874, he changed it to *Misumena pustulosa*, and it has since been changed to its present name, *Thomisus spectabilis*. This represents only one of the many problems confronting a student of this interesting section of our fauna. Body length: male 6.2mm, female 10mm. Colour: as illustrated. Identification: by photograph. Egg-sac: in folded end of leaf, 14mm in diameter, eggs in centre section, sac of very white silk, with smooth surface. Eggs: 1mm in diameter, cream in colour, with a frosted appearance, non-glutinous, 200–370 in number. Dimorphism: male smaller than female. Food: other spiders and small insects. Specimen: No. 77 (female), from Maleny, Queensland.

Crab Spider *Runcinia elongata*

Another species which has had a change of name. L. Koch described this spider in 1874 under the name *Misumena elongata*, which was later changed to its present name. Originally listed as a Queensland spider, it is quite common in New South Wales, particularly in the Sydney area. It is usually found in grass-seeding heads and low herbage, and builds no web-snare. The egg-sac is built in the seeding heads of grass, and the female sits on the sac until the eggs hatch, and if removed, will run straight back to the sac when released. Body length: male 4mm, female 9mm. Colour: varies from almost white, to deep red; the common colour is illustrated. Identification: by photograph. Egg-sac: 10mm in diameter, of very white silk, camouflaged with grass-seeds and debris. Eggs: 0.9mm in diameter, translucent, cream in colour, non-glutinous, 40–60 in number. Dimorphism: male much smaller than female in the body, legs about equal in length. Food: small insects which are attracted to grass-seeding heads, predominantly small moths. Specimen: No. 78 (female), from Royal National Park, Audley, Sydney.

75

76

77

78

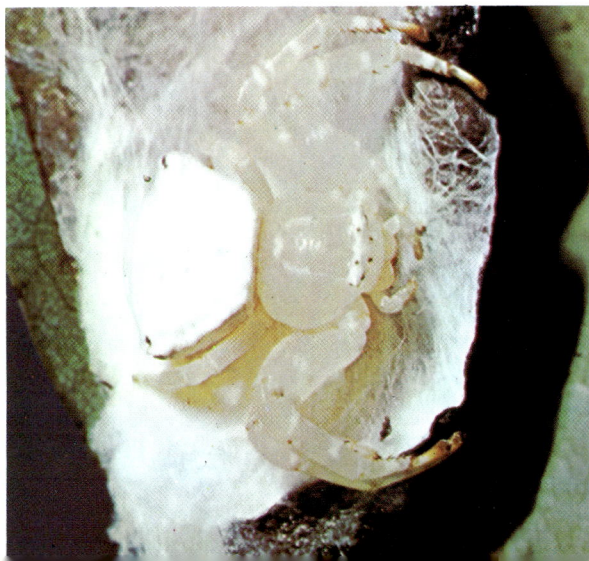

Flower Spider *Diaea insecta*

Though many of these spiders frequent flowers, some species appear to favour cones and seed-cases of native plants. Some species which do prefer flowers may be variable in colour, and usually adapt to some degree the colour of the flower. No web-snare is built by any of these spiders; food is captured by grasping with legs one and two, which are always much longer than the others. Body length: male 3mm, female unknown to the author. Colour: as illustrated. Identification: by photograph. Egg-sac and eggs: unknown. Dimorphism: male probably smaller than female. Food: small insects. Specimens: No. 79 (male), from Wilton, New South Wales.

Flower Spider *Diaea prasina*

This species was found on flowers of *Senecio species*, and though the flowers were yellow in colour, the spider was very hard to detect. Body length: male 4.5mm, female 6mm. Colour: as illustrated. Identification: by photograph. Egg-sac and eggs: unknown to author. Dimorphism: male slightly smaller, though similar to female. Food: small insects attracted to the flowers. Specimen: No. 80 (female), from Royal National Park, Audley, Sydney.

Flower Spider *Diaea evanida*

A small but beautiful species, about the commonest of this genus. It is found in most gardens, particularly in the Sydney area, if shrubs and flowers are present. It ranges through to Queensland, and possibly as far south as Melbourne. Body length: male 5mm, female 7mm. Colour: variable, from white to deep yellow. Identification: by dorsal pattern on the abdomen. Egg-sac: usually on the underside of a leaf, 6mm in diameter, of white, shiny silk. Eggs: 0.8mm in diameter, a translucent, creamy colour, 20–40 in number; the mother guards the sac. Dimorphism: male slightly smaller than female. Food: other small spiders and insects. Specimen: No. 81 (female), from Botany, Sydney.

Flower Spider *Diaea albiceris*

Though the author can find no record of this species being found in New South Wales, this specimen was collected from this State. It was described by L. Koch in 1876, and since then there appears to have been no work done on the species. Body length: male unknown to the author, female 7mm. Colour: as illustrated. Identification: by dorsal pattern on the abdomen. Egg-sac: 8mm long, 6mm wide at its widest point, of fine, white silk, thicker in the centre. Eggs: 0.7mm in diameter, translucent white, 42 in number. Dimorphism: unknown. Food: small spiders and insects. Specimen: No. 82 (female), from Richmond, New South Wales.

Plate 21
79. *Diaea insecta* (male)
80. *Diaea prasina* (female)
81. *Diaea evanida* (female)
82. *Diaea albiceris* (female) with sac

79

80

81

82

Flower Spider *Diaea pilula*

This species has been known as *Xysticus pilula* since L. Koch described it in 1874. In 1966 Dr C. D. Dondale placed the species in the genus *Diaea*. As the holotype is missing from the Hamburg Museum in Germany, and this species fits the key to the genus *Diaea*, the author agrees with Dr Dondale in his decision to alter it. Body length: male 3mm, female 4.3mm. Colour: as illustrated, though male has two dark bars on the carapace. Identification: by photograph and dorsal pattern on the abdomen. Egg-sac: fastened in a folded leaf, round in shape, 5mm in diameter, eggs in centre, sac of white silk. Eggs: 0.7mm in diameter, deep cream in colour, 27 in number. Dimorphism: male slightly smaller than female. Food: tiny insects. Specimen: No. 83 (female), from Royal National Park, Audley, Sydney.

Flower Spider *Diaea rosea*

The most beautiful of all *Diaeas*, this tiny spider is well-named, for the rose-red colour on the abdomen is outstanding. Hundreds of these spiders were found by the author on flowering Christmas Bells, *Blandfordia nobilis*, in Barren Grounds Faunal Reserve, Kiama, New South Wales. Though the spiders were plentiful, they were difficult to detect, owing to the colour harmony between flowers and spiders. As is the case with most Thomisids, the female guards the egg-sac, and cannot be encouraged to leave it. Body length: male 3mm, female 5.5mm. Colour: as illustrated, though some specimens have darker red on the abdomen than others. Identification: by dorsal pattern on the abdomen, and photograph. Egg-sac: usually built in seeding-heads of sedges, which grow in and around swamps. Sac is 6mm in diameter, round, of very white silk and camouflaged with debris. Eggs: 0.6mm in diameter, opaque pink in colour, 25–30 in number. Dimorph-

ism: male slimmer and smaller than female, slightly longer in legs. Food: very small insects. Specimen: No. 84 (female), from Barren Grounds Faunal Reserve, Kiama, New South Wales.

Flower Spider *Diaea variabilis*

This is a fairly widespread species in eastern Australia, and is often found on white flowers, particularly Flannel Flowers, *Actinotus helianthi*. Like *D. evanida* (No. 81), it is common in gardens in and around Sydney. Body length: male 5mm, female 7mm. Colour: as illustrated. Identification: by photograph. Egg-sac: 9mm long, 6mm wide, of white silk, usually under a leaf. Eggs: 0.8mm in diameter, pale cream in colour, non-glutinous, 25–30 in number. Dimorphism: male smaller, but similar to female. Food: small insects and other spiders. Specimen: No. 85 (female), from Botany, Sydney.

Crab Spider *Xysticus bilimbatus*

A small spider, which is apparently restricted to New South Wales, and is a rare species. The author knows nothing of its field habits. Body length: male 3mm, female 5mm. Colour: as illustrated. Egg-sac and eggs: unknown. Dimorphism: male smaller than female. Food: very small insects. Specimen: No. 86 (female), from Middle Cove, Sydney.

Plate 22
83. *Diaea pilula* (female)
84. *Diaea rosea* (female) with sac
85. *Diaea variabilis* (female) with sac
86. *Xysticus bilimbatus* (female)

83

84

85

86

Crab Spider *Hedana valida*

An obscure species of Thomisid, which owing to its nocturnal habits, is seldom seen by the public. Usually inhabiting rain-forest, it builds no web-snare, and is found sitting on the under-surface of leaves during the day. The green colouring of this spider makes it almost impossible to detect when sitting still under a leaf. At night it is sometimes found hanging from a single thread of silk, about 15cm long. Body length: male 4mm, female 5mm. Colour: as illustrated. Identification: by photograph. Egg-sac and eggs: unknown. Dimorphism: male more slender than female. Food: mostly tiny moths. Specimen: No. 87 (female), from Royal National Park, Audley, Sydney.

Crab Spider *Stephanopis barbipes*

This minute spider was described by Keyserling in 1883 from a male collected in Cape York. It is fairly common in the Sydney area, and also occurs in Tasmania. It is usually found among dead ferns in heavily timbered country, or in litter among the trees. Body length: male 3mm, female 5mm. Colour: as illustrated. Egg-sac and eggs: unknown to the author. Identification: by photograph, and the patch of heavy bristles on tibia of leg one. Dimorphism: male smaller and slimmer than female, bristles lacking on leg one of the female. Food: small insects. Specimen: No. 88 (male), from Ku-ring-gai Chase National Park, Sydney.

Crab Spider *Stephanopis obtusifrons*

Many species of *Stephanopis* are difficult to locate, for they build no web-snare, and inhabit the bark of trees. The spider usually matches the bark of the tree in texture and colour, and it is only when the spider moves that it can be seen. This species is mostly found on the bark of *Angophoras*, though one or two have been collected from the bark of other trees. New South Wales and Victoria appear to be the only States in which this spider is found, though it does not seem to be plentiful in any area. Body length: male 6mm, female 8mm. Colour: as illustrated. Identification: by photograph, and pattern on dorsal surface of the abdomen. Egg-sac and eggs: unknown. Dimorphism: male smaller than female. Food: bark-dwelling insects, and possibly other spiders. Specimen: No. 89 (female), from Eltham, Victoria.

Crab Spider *Stephanopis scabra*

Melanic forms have been found of several species in this genus. These forms are usually found on burnt trees, or on trees with black bark. The specimen shown is an exception, for it was found on light bark, guarding its egg-sac. Body length: male 6mm, female 9mm. Colour: normally from light to dark grey. Egg-sac: 7.5mm in diameter, irregular in shape, usually placed in a crevice in the bark and camouflaged with debris of a fine nature. Eggs: about 1mm in diameter, translucent off-white in colour, 25–35 in number. Dimorphism: male smaller than female. Food: other spiders are the only food observed by the author, Salticidae and Hersiliidae are the only families seen being eaten. Specimen: No. 90 (female), from Ku-ring-gai Chase National Park, Sydney.

Plate 23
87. *Hedana valida* (female)
88. *Stephanopis barbipes* (male)
89. *Stephanopis obtusifrons* (female)
90. *Stephanopis scabra* (female) with sac

87

88

89

90

Crab Spider *Stephanopis cambridgei*

This is a widespread species, being found from Queensland to Tasmania. It is usually found on or under eucalypt bark, as are most of this genus. Most Stephanopids sit with legs one and two folded tightly to the body, whereas this species and *S. obtusifrons* sit with legs one and two stretched straight out in front of the body. This spider is also the largest in the genus, some of them being quite tiny. Thorell described this species in 1870, and doubted whether it really fitted into the genus *Stephanopis*. It is closer to *Synalus* (No. 94) in habits than it is to *Stephanopis*. Body length: male 7–8mm, female 10–11mm. Colour: variable, from grey to rich brown, though brown is the commonest colour. This depends on the colour of the bark it is living on. Identification: by photograph and legs stretched out in front. Egg-sac: usually in a leaf with the tip folded back to cover the eggs, the leaf being fastened to the branch with silk, so it will not fall. The sac is flat on the edges, and raised in the centre where the eggs are. Eggs: unknown to the author. Dimorphism: male smaller and more slender than the female. Food: other spiders and insects. Specimens: Nos 91 and 92 (male and female), from Royal National Park, Audley, Sydney.

Crab Spider *Stephanopis corticalis*

This species appears to be confined to western New South Wales and Queensland, and can be considered a rare spider. The species was described by L. Koch in 1875, the specimen being collected at Gayndah in Queensland. There does not appear to have been anything written about this spider since. It is a bark-dwelling species, usually inhabiting the bark of eucalypts, and sits with legs one and two folded tightly to the body. Body length: male 5mm, female 8mm. Colour: as illustrated. Identification: by photograph. Egg-sac and eggs: unknown.

Dimorphism: male smaller than female, though similar in appearance. Food: probably small insects. Specimen: No. 93 (female), from Mount Wilson, Blue Mountains, New South Wales.

Crab Spider *Synalus angustus*

This is another obscure species which was described by L. Koch in 1876, but from then on its life has been a closed book. It appears to be confined to the Sydney area, though one other species is described from Tasmania. These are the only species in the genus, *S. angustus* being the type of the genus. This spider builds no web-snare; it captures its food by grasping it with legs one and two. Its habit of lying along a twig with legs one and two stretched out in front of the body makes it almost impossible to detect. Occasionally it is found at night, hanging from a single strand of silk about 5cm long. Body length: male 7mm, female 11mm. Colour: always the same as the twig it is found on. Identification: by the elongated body, which is cut off square on the posterior end. Egg-sac and eggs: unknown. Dimorphism: male smaller and slimmer than female. Food: a wide variety of insects. Specimen: No. 94 (female), from Royal National Park, Audley, Sydney.

Plate 24
91. *Stephanopis cambridgei* (male)
92. *Stephanopis cambridgei* (female)
93. *Stephanopis corticalis* (female)
94. *Synalus angustus* (female)

91

92

93

94

Crab Spider *Sidymella rubrosignata*

The genus *Sidymella* is another confusing one, with some naturalists using the name *Sidyma* for the genus. Simon erected the genus in 1895, but the name *Sidyma* had already been taken by an insect (Walker 1856). Strand renamed the genus *Sidymella*, which the rules of nomenclature allow, so the author uses the latter. Most species in this genus have trapezium-shaped abdomens, and sit with legs one and two extended straight out in front of the body, making them easily identifiable. Like all other Thomisids, these spiders do not build a web-snare, and usually sit quite still, waiting for their prey to come to them, making sightings difficult. To make matters worse, the colour of the spider usually matches the surrounds; this species is mostly found on green shrubs or trees. Body length: male 4.5mm, female 8mm. Colour: mostly green, though the author has collected specimens from yellow flowers which were a deep brownish-yellow in colour. Identification: by the photograph. Egg-sac: always in a leaf, the tip of which has been folded back to cover the eggs, and the edges brought together to form a retreat (see No. 96). Eggs: 0.8mm in diameter, cream in colour, non-glutinous, 20–35 in number. Dimorphism: male much slimmer, smaller, and longer in the legs than the female. Food: a wide variety of small insects, and occasionally other small spiders. Specimens: Nos 95 and 96 (male and female), from Royal National Park, Audley, Sydney.

Crab Spider *Sidymella species*

This unusual species is probably undescribed, and it was only after many hours of studying the specimens that the author was convinced that this species belongs to the genus *Sidymella*. It is apparently restricted to the Sydney area, and several specimens have been taken on the northern side of Sydney Harbour. Each specimen found has been sitting in the typical *Sidymella* position, and its general habits conform with that genus, as do its general characteristics other than the abdomen. Body length: male 8mm, female 12mm. Colour: as illustrated. Identification: by photograph. Egg-sac and eggs: unknown. Food: small moths and insects. Specimen: No. 97 (female), from Turramurra, Sydney.

Crab Spider *Sidymella lobata*

A tiny species, which is found in New South Wales and Queensland. Though common in New South Wales, it is seldom recorded. This is probably due to its small size, and its habit of living in litter and debris close to the ground in semi-rain-forest, or closely timbered areas. Body length: male 3mm, female 4mm. Colour: from light brown to almost black. Identification: by its size, and the photograph. Egg-sac and eggs: unknown to the author. Food: tiny insects which inhabit forest litter and debris. Dimorphism: male similar to, but slightly smaller than female. Specimen: No. 98 (female), from Royal National Park, Audley, Sydney.

Plate 25
95. *Sidymella rubrosignata* (male)
96. *Sidymella rubrosignata* (female) with sac
97. *Sidymella species* (female)
98. *Sidymella lobata* (female)

95

96

97

98

Crab Spider *Sidymella hirsuta*
This small spider was described by L. Koch in 1873, and little more is known about it now than was known then. This species can be considered a rare one, and appears to be restricted to New South Wales and Queensland. An astonishing feature of this spider was the fact that of the five specimens found by the author, four were found on a hairy plant, Wild Tobacco, *Solanum mauritiana*, the camouflage in each case was perfect. Body length: male 4mm, female 6mm. Colour: usually a creamy colour to match the stem of the Wild Tobacco plant. Identification: by its hairy appearance, and photograph. Egg-sac and eggs: unknown. Dimorphism: male smaller than the female. Food: small insects attracted to the above-mentioned plant. Specimen: No. 99 (female), from Gosford, New South Wales.

Crab Spider *Sidymella bicuspidata*
Another rare species of this genus, which was also described by L. Koch in 1873, from a specimen collected in Queensland. It probably ranges from Sydney to Queensland, for the author has found it in two localities in the Sydney area. The female folds a leaf into a retreat, which is shaped like a bell tent, and which acts as a nursery once she has mated. Unlike other such retreats, this species places a copious layer of white silk on the outside of the retreat. Body length: male unknown, female 7mm. Colour: as illustrated. Identification: by photograph. Egg-sac: always in the retreat, of very white silk, attached to side of retreat, flat, raised in the centre where eggs are, 8mm in diameter. Eggs: 0.8mm in diameter, a translucent dark brown in colour, non-glutinous, 40 in number. Dimorphism: unknown. Food: small insects. Specimen: No. 100 (female), from Beecroft, Sydney.

Crab Spider *Sidymella longipes*
This spider is probably the commonest species in the genus. It is frequently found in gardens in the Sydney area, and extends through to Queensland. Body length: male 5mm, female 8mm. Colour: as illustrated. Identification: by photograph. Egg-sac: usually in a partially curled leaf, sac of very white, shiny silk, about 6mm in diameter. Eggs: 0.8mm in diameter, cream in colour, 20–30 in number. Dimorphism: male smaller and slimmer than female. Food: small insects and other small spiders. Specimen: No. 101 (female), from Botany, Sydney.

Crab Spider *Sidymella trapezia*
This species is sometimes mistaken for the previous species; it is smaller than *S. longipes*, darker on the abdomen, with a lighter stripe down either side. It is widespread in its distribution, being found in Eastern Australia, and Western Australia. Body length: male 4mm, female 6mm. Colour: as illustrated. Identification: by photograph. Egg-sac and eggs: unknown to the author. Dimorphism: male slimmer and smaller than female. Food: small insects, and probably small spiders. Specimen: No. 102 (female), from Royal National Park, Audley, Sydney.

Plate 26
 99. *Sidymella hirsuta* (female)
100. *Sidymella bicuspidata* (female) with sac
101. *Sidymella longipes* (female)
102. *Sidymella trapezia* (female)

99

100

101

102

Crab Spider *Sidymella species*

At first glance this spider could be mistaken for a *Monaeses species*, but microscopic examination and careful checking prove otherwise. The genus *Sidymella* is apparently much larger than was thought, for six new species have been found in the past two years, all in the suburbs of Sydney. With the rapid development which is taking place all round our cities, no doubt many new species will be lost to science before they are discovered, as many of these spiders have restricted habitats, some of them restricted to only a few miles. Body length: male unknown, female 8mm. Colour: as illustrated. Identification: by photograph. Egg-sac and eggs: unknown. Dimorphism: male probably smaller than female. Food: this specimen readily ate flies, so the food probably consists of insects. Specimen: No. 103 (female), from East Gordon, Sydney.

FAMILY LINYPHIIDAE

Tent Spider *Linyphia species*

This is a rather complex family. The spiders are small and many of the species are similar in appearance, which leads to much confusion in identification. Many species build a sheet web, which is drawn up into a cone in the centre. At the apex of the cone there is usually a tent-like retreat, which is covered with debris and leaf litter. The spider is found in this retreat most of the time, and it is used as a nursery after the female has mated. The sheet web has a labyrinth of supporting threads surrounding it. Insects hitting this labyrinth, fall onto the sheet web, and are dragged through it by the spider, which moves on its underside. Body length: male unknown, female 5.4mm. Colour: as illustrated. Identification: by web and photograph. Egg-sac: 4.5mm in diameter, of fine, green silk. Eggs: 0.6mm in diameter, yellow-green in colour, 35–50 in number. Dimorphism: unknown. Food: small flying insects. Specimen: No. 104 (female), from Pittwater, Sydney.

FAMILY THERIDIIDAE

Whip Spider *Ariamnes colubrinus*

Dr Levi of Harvard University is of the opinion that this genus is synonymous with the genus *Argyrodes* (personal correspondence). The author agrees, but will not alter it until authoritatively informed of such a move. These spiders are quite common in New South Wales and Queensland, but owing to their habit of sitting quite still in their few strands of web are seldom seen. Body length: male 13mm, female 22mm. Colour: variable, from cream to dark green. Identification: by photograph and size. Egg-sac: 4mm x 3mm, with a small lip on the bottom, suspended from a stiff thread in the web. Eggs: 0.7mm in diameter, pale yellowish-green in colour, 40–50 in number. Dimorphism: male smaller and slimmer than female. Food: small insects, and occasionally other spiders. Specimens: Nos 105 and 106 (females), from Royal National Park, Audley, Sydney.

Plate 27
103. *Sidymella species* (female)
104. *Linyphia species* (female) with sac
105. *Ariamnes colubrinus* (female) with sac
106. *Ariamnes colubrinus* (female) with young

103

104

105

106

No common name *Phoroncidia sextuberculata*
This species was described by Keyserling in 1890, as *Ulesanis sextuberculata*. It has since been found that the genus *Ulesanis* is synonymous with *Phoroncidia*, and as *Phoroncidia* was erected in 1834 and *Ulesanis* in 1872, the former takes preference under the rules of nomenclature. These tiny spiders are seldom seen, as they appear to build no web-snare, just a single strand of silk, on which the spider rests at night. During daylight hours they sit with legs tightly folded, usually on a twig at the end of the web-strand. Body length: male unknown, female 2.5mm. Colour: as illustrated. Identification: by six tubercular projections on the abdomen. Egg-sac: unknown. Eggs: unknown. Dimorphism: male smaller than female, if this species is like other known ones. Food: tiny flying insects. Specimen: No. 107 (female), from Cordeaux Dam, New South Wales.

No common name *Euryopis superba*
These spiders are sometimes mistaken for ticks, owing to the very small legs compared with the body size. They are usually found under eucalypt bark, and this species is found in New South Wales and Victoria. Body length: male 2.7mm, female 5.2mm. Colour: as illustrated. Identification: by photograph and body shape. Egg-sac: about 6mm in diameter, of white, fluffy silk, usually under bark; the spider stays with sac until the young emerge. Eggs: 0.7mm in diameter, cream in colour, non-glutinous. Dimorphism: male identical to female, other than smaller size. Food: small bark-dwelling insects. Specimen: No. 108 (female), from Parramatta, New South Wales.

No common name *Theridion pyramidale*
This spider is probably the most beautiful of the Theridions, for most of this genus are rather drab in appearance. The web-snares of these spiders are irregular tangles, forming no set pattern. Many of them have a number of vertical strands descending from the tangle which have viscid drops on them. When these are touched they fly up, entangling the victim with the viscid drops. Body length: male 2.3mm, female 4mm. Colour: as illustrated, some specimens brighter than others. Identification: by pyramid-shaped abdomen. Egg-sac: spherical, 2.5-mm in diameter, suspended in web or fastened to a leaf at its edge. Eggs: 0.3mm in diameter, pale cream in colour, 40–50 in number. Dimorphism: male smaller than female. Food: small insects and ants. Specimen: No. 109 (female), from Turramurra, Sydney.

Dew-drop Spider *Argyrodes antipodianus*
These silver midgets do not build a web of their own, but live in the webs of other spiders. They are often found in large *Nephila* webs, as these specimens were. Body length: male 2.5mm, female 3mm. Colour: as illustrated. Identification: by photograph. Egg-sac: as in photograph, 3mm in length, suspended on strong thread. Eggs: 0.3mm in diameter, white in colour, 20–35 in number. Dimorphism: male smaller and much slimmer than female. Food: small insects caught in web of host spider. Specimen: No. 110 (male and female), from Ku-ring-gai Chase National Park, Sydney.

Plate 28
107. *Phoroncidia sextuberculata* (female)
108. *Euryopis superba* (female)
109. *Theridion pyramidale* (female) with sac
110. *Argyrodes antipodianus* (male *left* and female *right*) with sacs

107

108

109

110

Red and Black Spider *Nicodamus bicolor*

L. Koch described this spider under the name *Centropelma Ꝑbicolor*, in 1872. The name *Centropelma* was found to be preoccupied, so it was given its present name. The genus has been placed in three distinct families by various authors, and its true taxonomic position is still not certain. Of the three families it has been placed in, Theridiidae, Agelenidae and Zodariidae, the present author prefers to leave it in the family Theridiidae. The reason for this is the fact that two species were described as Theridions by prominent arachnologists, and its habits are closer to this family than the others. The bright contrasting colours of these spiders, plus the fact that they are widespread and common, attract much interest.

They are usually found under loose bark, stones, logs and fallen trees, always close to the ground. The web consists of a few irregular strands, built horizontally, the spider moving on the underside. Body length: male 10mm, female 12mm. Colour: as illustrated. Identification: by photograph, colour, and size. Egg-sac: plano-convex, of white, flocculent silk, usually under bark. Eggs: 1mm in diameter, pale cream in colour, 30–50 in number. Dimorphism: male almost the same size as female. Specimen: Nos 111 and 112 (male and female), from Kurnell, Sydney.

Red and Black Spider *Nicodamus dimidiatus*

This small species was described by E. Simon in 1897, and though similar in colour to the previous species, is very much smaller. The web and habits are similar to the other members of the genus, and it is usually found under bark lying on the ground, or under debris and leaf litter among trees. Body length: male 2.5mm, female 3mm. Colour: as illustrated. Identification: by photograph and size. Egg-sac: a tiny, fluffy ball of white silk, 3mm in diameter, usually attached to bark. Eggs: 0.4mm in diameter, cream in colour, 10–20 in number. Dimorphism: male similar to, though slightly smaller than female. Food: tiny insects. Specimen: No. 113 (male), from Springwood, New South Wales.

Red and Black Spider *Nicodamus semiflavum*

A widespread species from Eastern Australia generally, which was described by L. Koch in 1872. The carapace of this species is more yellow than red, as are the legs, though some specimens are darker. This is another common species, but being smaller than *N. bicolor*, does not attract as much attention as does the larger species. Commonly found under bark, either on the tree, or on the ground, usually in a shady position, as is the case with the other species. Body length: male 3.5mm, female 5mm. Colour: variable, from yellowish-red to bright red on the carapace, abdomen blue-black. Identification: by photograph and size. Egg-sac: plano-convex, of white, flocculent silk, usually attached to bark, some times hung in web. Eggs: 0.8mm in diameter, light cream in colour, 25–40 in number, non-glutinous. Dimorphism: male slightly smaller than female. Food: small insects. Specimen: No. 114 (female), from Hartley, New South Wales.

Plate 29
111. *Nicodamus bicolor* (male)
112. *Nicodamus bicolor* (female)
113. *Nicodamus dimidiatus* (male)
114. *Nicodamus semiflavum* (female)

111

112

113

114

Red-back Spider *Latrodectus hasselti*
This poisonous spider is a geographic variant of the dreaded Black Widow Spider of America. Up to 1959 there were at least thirteen deaths from bites of the Red-back Spider in Australia. There were probably many more, as many deaths were recorded as, "effects of spider bite", "venomous bite", "possibly a spider bite", and so on. A specific antivenene for the bite of this species was produced in the Serum Laboratories at Parkville, in Victoria, and became available in 1956. The female is the deadly sex in this species. The male, a tiny individual with black and white stripes on the body, would not be recognised as the mate to the conspicuous female. Rubbish, litter, old tins and containers in the yard of a home will encourage the breeding of this spider.

Body length: male 4mm, female 10mm. Colour: female as illustrated: male, white abdomen with four black bars on either side. Identification: female by photograph. Egg-sac: spherical, up to 10mm in diameter, of strong, yellow-brown silk, usually four or five in number. Eggs: off-white colour, varying in number from 50 to over 200. Dimorphism: male very much smaller and different in colour from female. Food: usually insects of a wide range, occasionally small skinks. Specimen: No. 115 (female), from Canberra.

No common name *Phylarchus splendens*
This small species named by William Rainbow in 1916 was placed in the genus *Phylarchus* with a query. Since then no work has been done on this species. It appears to be restricted to the Sydney area, and is usually found under stones. Body length: male 4.5mm, female 5.5mm. Colour: as illustrated. Identification: by photograph. Egg-sac: spherical or nearly so, 5mm in diameter, of very white, fluffy silk, suspended from or fastened to underside of rock. Eggs: 0.5mm in diameter, deep cream in colour, 18–25 in number, non-glutinous. Dimorphism: male much slimmer than female, though similar in colour. Food: small ground-dwelling insects. Specimen: No. 116 (female), from Royal National Park, Audley, Sydney.

FAMILY ARGIOPIDAE

Long-jawed Spider *Tetragnatha bituberculata*
The spiders of this very large family, are varied in form and habit; among them are the orb-weavers, and some which build no web-snare at all. This species is usually found near creeks, sometimes the orb web is stretched over a creek. It is found in New South Wales and Queensland. The genus is a large one, containing seventeen species, and can be identified by the long jaws, which protrude in front of the cephalothorax. Body length: male 10mm, female 14mm. Colour: as illustrated. Identification: by long jaws and two tubercules on the abdomen, one on either side. Egg-sac: 3.5mm in diameter, granulated surface, suspended by strong guy-threads of silk. Eggs: 1mm in diameter, white to off-white in colour, 27 in number. Dimorphism: male slightly smaller and slimmer than female. Food: small flying insects. Specimens: Nos 117 and 118 (female and egg sacs), from Minnamurra Falls Reserve, Kiama, New South Wales.

Plate 30
115. *Latrodectus hasselti* (female)
116. *Phylarchus splendens* (female) with sac
117. *Tetragnatha bituberculata* (female)
118. *Tetragnatha bituberculata* (egg-sacs)

115

116

↑

117

118

Two-spined Spider *Poecilopachys bispinosa*
This is one of the many beautiful species in the family Argiopidae. The colour in this species varies considerably from one specimen to another. A remarkable feature of this spider is the way in which the colour seems to pulsate on the outer surface, particularly when the spider is agitated, bringing about a complete colour change in the spider. First described by Keyserling in 1865 under the name *Cytarachne bispinosa*, it was later changed to its present genus. It builds a small orb web, and the spider is usually found in the centre of the orb. Body length: male 2mm, female 6mm. Colour: as illustrated. Identification: by two large, white spines on the abdomen. Egg-sac: spindle-shaped, 24mm long, outer covering of brown, papery silk, mostly surrounded by a tangle of web. Eggs: 0.8mm in diameter, cream in colour, 45–70 in number. Dimorphism: male is tiny replica of female. Food: small flying insects. Specimen: No. 119 (female), from Royal National Park, Audley, Sydney.

Bird-dropping Spider *Celaenia kinbergi*
This spider is a master of camouflage, and when it sits on a leaf with all legs folded tightly to its body it is overlooked more than it is noticed. It builds no web-snare, but captures its food by grasping it with legs one and two. When in the feeding position, it hangs head down, with legs one and two spread widely, ready to grasp any moth which approaches. To feed it usually hangs from the edge of a leaf, or the egg-sacs. This species is commonly found on fruit trees, and is sometimes called the Orchard Spider. As *Celaenia kinbergi* lives entirely on moths, it does a lot of good in keeping down these pests among fruit trees. Body length: male 2.5mm, female 12mm. Colour: from black and white to dirty brown. Identification: by photograph. Egg-

sac: spherical, 12–14mm in diameter, of dark brown, papery silk, with black criss-cross markings on the outer covering. Usually hanging in an elongated bunch, numbering up to 13. Eggs: 1mm in diameter, a translucent-yellow in colour, 150–200 in number, non-glutinous. Dimorphism: male very much smaller than female. Food: moths of several species. Specimen: No. 120 (female), from Botany, Sydney.

Leaf-curling Spider *Phonognatha graeffei*
This species was described by Keyserling in 1865 as *Epeira graeffei*. In 1894, Simon described it as *Phonognatha graeffei*, and in 1896 Rainbow described it as *Epeira wagneri*. Dr Dondale cleared the matter up in 1966, and the name now stands at *Phonognatha graeffei*, and the other names become synonyms. This spider is probably the best-known species of our spiders, being of widespread distribution, and easily recognised by its habit of using a curled leaf for its retreat. The retreat is placed in the centre of the web. The eggs are placed in a folded leaf, and suspended up to 4m from the web. Body length: male 5mm, female 8mm. Colour: as illustrated. Identification: by photograph, and curled leaf in web. Egg-sac: in a folded leaf, oval, 10mm x 8mm, of fluffy, cream silk. Eggs: 0.8mm in diameter, pale cream in colour, 150–200 in number, glutinous. Dimorphism: male slightly smaller than female. Food: insects. Specimen: No. 121 (female), from Ku-ring-gai Chase National Park, Sydney.

Plate 31
119. *Poecilopachys bispinosa* (female)
120. *Celaenia kinbergi* (female) with sacs
121. *Phonognatha graeffei* (female)
122. *Phonognatha graeffei* (egg-sac)

119

120

121

122

Golden Orb-weaving Spider *Nephila ornata*

The Nephilas are well known for their huge golden orb-webs, and the large size of the spiders. The golden silk of the webs is remarkably strong, and occasionally small birds get caught when they blunder into the webs. The fact that small birds are sometimes caught does not mean the spiders eat them; in fact this is doubtful. The author has found large cicadas being eaten by this species, but never birds. Aggregates of webs belonging to this species are sometimes found among mangrove trees, and along the banks of tidal creeks. Rainbow described this species in 1896 from specimens collected in the Sydney area, and this spider appears to be restricted to Sydney and its suburbs. Body length: male 5mm, female 20mm. Colour: as illustrated. Identification: by photograph. Egg-sac: 4cm x 3cm, roughly oval in shape, of bright yellow silk, usually camouflaged with leaves or debris. Built among foliage near outer edges of web. Eggs: 1mm in diameter, of a deep golden colour, with a whitish frosting covering them. Several hundred in number, non-glutinous. Dimorphism: male so small in comparison, that he is often overlooked. Food: flying insects, even to large cicadas. Specimen: Nos 123 and 124, from Malabar, Sydney.

Golden Orb-weaving Spider *Nephila maculata*

This species is the largest of the Nephilas, and has the widest distribution of the genus. It is found in India, Malaysia, Papua, New Guinea, Polynesia and Northern Queensland. This species is the type of the genus, and was described by Fabricius in 1793. There are two varieties, *N. maculata* var. *penicillum*, and *N. maculata* var. *walckenaerii;* both are found in North Queensland. This spider builds an enormous golden web, and as with the previous species, these are often found in aggregates. Some of these webs are strung between trees up to 20m from the ground. The spider is also quite large, and may have a leg span of up to 19cm; it is not known to be harmful to man.

The silken web of this spider is extremely strong, and the inhabitants of some Pacific islands have used it for several purposes for many years. In parts of New Guinea, the local people make fishing scoop nets from it. In another part of New Guinea, they make a smothering mask from the silk, which is used to smother the guilty in adultery cases. Body length: male unknown to the author, female 4cm. Colour: as illustrated. Identification: by the size, and photograph. Egg-sac: unknown to the author, as are the eggs. Dimorphism: unknown. Food: large flying insects, particularly cicadas. Specimen: No. 125 (female), from Cooktown, North Queensland. Specimen: No. 126 (immature female), from Tully, North Queensland. *Note:* This immature stage was described as a different species by L. Koch in 1871; he named it *N. sulphurosa*.

Plate 32
123. *Nephila ornata* (female)
124. *Nephila ornata* (male and female)
125. *Nephila maculata* (female) mature
126. *Nephila maculata* (female) immature

123

124

125

126

Golden Orb-weaving Spider *Nephila edulis*
This spider was described by L. Koch in 1871, as *Nephila imperatrix*, it has since been changed to *N. edulis*. It is a widespread species, being found in New South Wales, Queensland, Western Australia, and the Great Barrier Reef. The golden orb web is usually built in low coastal scrub or small trees, and this spider does not appear to build high up as do many species of this genus. Body length: male 4–5mm, female 20–22mm. Colour: as illustrated. Identification: by the crescent-shaped lighter band on the anterior, dorsal aspect of the abdomen, and photograph. Egg-sac: roughly oval in shape, 4cm long, of bright yellow, looped silk, usually with some leaves fastened to the sac. Eggs: 1mm in diameter, bright yellow in colour, frosty appearance, 200–300 in number, non-glutinous. Dimorphism: male very much smaller than female. Food: flying insects. Specimen: No. 127 (female), from Huskisson, New South Wales.

No common name *Argiope trifasciata*
A widespread species, found on almost all coastal regions of the continent, in Tasmania, America, and Polynesia. This spider appears to favour reedy situations for its habitat. A stabilimentum is sometimes built in the web, though it does not seem to be the general practice. The egg-sac is usually built in foliage adjacent to the outskirts of the orb web, and is suspended among the leaves; normally only one sac is built. Body length: male 4mm, female 16–20mm. Colour: as illustrated, though sometimes the abdominal colours are a little brighter. Egg-sac; plano-convex, tapering towards the top, about 35–40mm in length, of brownish colour. Eggs: 1mm in diameter, pale cream in colour, 150–200 in number. Dimorphism: male very much smaller than female. Food: flying insects.

Specimens: Nos 128 and 129 (females), from Jenolan Caves, New South Wales.

Tear-drop Spider *Argiope protensa*
This beautiful little spider is found all over Australia and in New Zealand. It is commonly found in tall grasses and low herbage, and the orb web may be inclined or horizontal. A ragged stabilimentum is sometimes present. It was described by L. Koch in 1871, and though several authors state that *A. syrmatica* is synonymous with this species, this is wrong. Body length: male 3mm, female 15mm. Identification: by photograph. Colour: as illustrated. Egg-sac: cup-shaped, top flat, 5mm in diameter. Eggs: 0.8mm in diameter, cream in colour, 30–40 in number, non-glutinous. Dimorphism: male smaller and shorter in abdomen. Food: small flying insects of a wide variety. Specimen: No. 130 (female), from Botany, Sydney.

Plate 33
127. *Nephila edulis* (female)
128. *Argiope trifasciata* (female)
129. *Argiope trifasciata* (female) building sac
130. *Argiope protensa* (female)

127

128

129

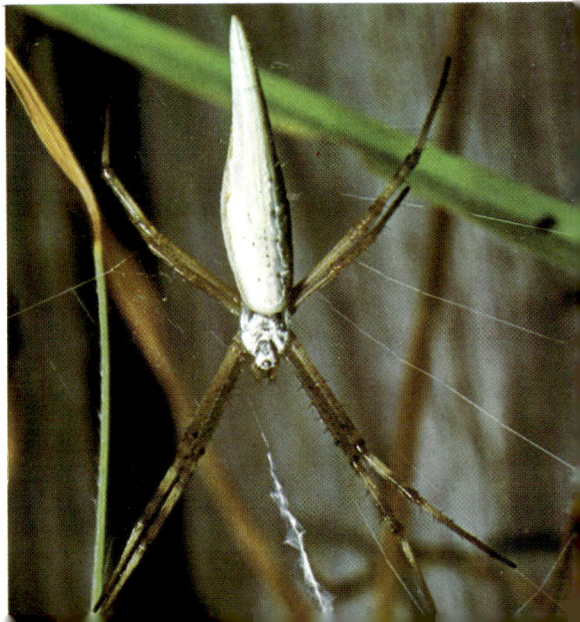

130

Saint Andrew's Cross Spider *Argiope aetherea*
Probably one of the best-known spiders in Australia, this species is known for its bright colours, and its spectacular web. It was described by Walckenaer in 1837 as *Epeira aetherea*, and altered by him to its present name in 1865. The female builds a hackled cross, or stabilimentum, in the centre of its web. In the webs of immature females, this stabilimentum is a delicate tracery; when the spider is mature, the hackling is more solid in structure, and much thicker in texture. When these spiders are very small, they sometimes build a spiral stabilimentum in the centre of the tiny web. When adult, the female spider sits on the cross in a head-down position, with the legs in pairs, one pair to each of the four segments of the cross. The theoretic purposes of this stabilimentum are many and varied; as yet, not one has been proved.

When the spider is absent from the normal position on the cross, the web is quite noticeable, yet once the spider is back on the cross, the web is difficult to see. This tends towards the cross being a form of camouflage for the brightly-coloured spider, plus the fact that the sombre male does not build a stabilimentum in its web. The egg-sac is built in the foliage to which the web is attached; occasionally, two sacs are built. The mating of this species is a dangerous affair for the male, for apart from the disparity of size in the sexes, the female is vicious if she is not ready to mate. One pair observed by the author was a perfect example; the female was not ready for copulation, and the male lost three legs in his attempts to mate before he called it a day.

Body length: male 5mm, female 14mm. Colour: as illustrated. Identification: by photograph and stabilimentum in the web. Egg-sac: pear-shaped, plano-convex, 4cm long, 2cm wide at its widest point, dirty white to greenish in colour. Eggs: 0.8mm in diameter, an opaque light-brown in colour, in a glutinous mass, several hundred in number. Dimorphism: male much smaller and slimmer than female. Food: a wide variety of insects. Specimens: No. 131 (male), from Mascot, Sydney; No. 132 (female), from Botany, Sydney; No. 133 (female), from Ku-ring-gai Chase, Sydney.

No common name *Argiope extensa*
A smaller species, the habits of which are a closed book. It was described by W. Rainbow in 1897, from a female specimen collected at Guildford, New South Wales. This species would appear to be confined to New South Wales. Body length: male unknown, female 11mm. Colour: as illustrated. Identification: by photograph. Egg-sac: three in number, 6mm wide, 9mm long, oval in shape, of dirty-white silk, with green tufts scattered over surface. Eggs: 0.7mm in diameter, translucent yellow in colour, semi-glutinous, 50–60 in number. Dimorphism: unknown. Food: small flying insects. Specimen: No. 134 (female), from The Rock, New South Wales.

Plate 34
131. *Argiope aetherea* (male)
132. *Argiope aetherea* (female)
133. *Argiope aetherea* (female) with sac
134. *Argiope extensa* (female) with sacs

131

132

133

134

No common name *Argiope syrmatica*

This species was described by L. Koch in 1871, and is classed as being synonymous with No. 130, *A. protensa*, by many authors. After careful study of both species, this author is convinced that they are a distinct species, and should remain as such. The orb web of this species sometimes has an irregular stabilimentum in the centre; in some cases this is a single hackled band. This spider has a wide distribution, being found in Queensland, New South Wales, Victoria and New Zealand. The egg-sacs of this species are cup-shaped, and number up to nine. The sacs are supported by guy-lines of silk which are attached to the flat lid on the sac, and are usually found on the foliage to which the orb web is attached. Body length: male unknown, female 14mm. Colour: as illustrated. Identification: by photograph. Egg-sac: cup-shaped, 8mm in diameter, 10mm deep, flat on top, rounded on the bottom; of white, tough, papery silk, with green tufts attached to outer surface. Eggs: 1mm in diameter, translucent, deep yellow in colour, non-glutinous, 140 in number. Dimorphism: unknown, though male is probably much smaller than female. Food: flying insects. Specimen: No. 135 (female), from Springwood, New South Wales.

No common name *Gea theridioides*

This small spider does not appear to be plentiful anywhere, and though its distribution is Australia-wide, only odd specimens are found from time to time. It builds a small orb web, usually close to the ground, and the star-shaped egg-sac is suspended in the outskirts of the web. Body length: male unknown, female 6.5mm. Colour: as illustrated. Identification: by photograph. Egg-sac: star-shaped, thicker in the centre, tapering to the edges, 12mm long, of tough, papery, crenated silk. Eggs: unknown. Dimorphism: unknown. Food: small flying insects. Specimen: No. 137 (female), from Botany, Sydney.

No common name *Cyrtophora parnasia*

The genus *Cyrtophora* has only five species which are found in Australia; four of these are shown and discussed here. *C. parnasia* has a wide distribution, being found in Queensland, New South Wales, and Victoria. L. Koch described it in 1871 from specimens collected at Bowen, in Queensland. It builds a beautiful, fine web, which tapers to a cone at the top—like a bell tent. The cone usually has debris attached to the outside at the top which forms a retreat for the spider and also serves as a nursery. The egg-sac is built in this retreat. Body length: male 5mm, female 10mm. Colour: as illustrated. Identification: by its web and photograph. Egg-sac: plano-convex, 10mm in diameter, of greenish-white silk, with tufts of green attached to the outer surface. Eggs: 0.8mm in diameter, pale cream in colour, 45–60 in number, non-glutinous. Dimorphism: male smaller and slimmer than female. Food: small insects captured in the web. Specimen: No. 138 (female), from Mount Druitt, New South Wales.

Plate 35
135. *Argiope syrmatica* (female)
136. *Argiope syrmatica* (egg-sacs)
137. *Gea theridioides* (female) with sac
138. *Cyrtophora parnasia* (female) with sac

135

136

137

138

No common name *Cyrtophora crassipes*
This spider was described by W. Rainbow in 1897 as *Epeira crassipes*, which he later changed to *Araneus crassipes*. But after studying the species and the original description there is no doubt that it belongs to the genus *Cyrtophora*. Rainbow even described the unusual bell-tent web when he described the species, plus the retreat at the top of the cone. He described it from a specimen collected at Guildford, New South Wales. The author has studied and collected this species in the Sydney area. Body length: male 3.5mm, female 6mm. Colour: as illustrated. Identification: by photograph and the web. Egg-sac and eggs: unknown. Dimorphism: male smaller and slimmer than female. Food: small insects, including ants. Specimen: No. 139 (female), from Royal National Park, Audley, Sydney.

No common name *Cyrtophora moluccensis*
This species was first described by Doleschall in 1857 as *Epeira moluccensis*. Since then it has had a wide range of names, including the following: *Epeira margaritacea* (Doleschall), *Epeira maritima* (Keyserling), *Epeira cupidinea* (Thorell), and *Epeira hieroglyphica* (L. Koch). It is a very widespread species, being found in New Guinea, Torres Strait, Queensland, New South Wales, and Polynesia, which probably accounts for it being named so many times. Body length: male 4mm, female 15mm. Colour: as illustrated. Identification: by photograph. Egg-sac: pear-shaped, 2.5cm in length, 10–12mm wide at the widest point, of dirty-white silk, with light brown, flocculent patches on outer surface. Eggs: 1mm in diameter, creamy colour, non-glutinous, 130–160 in number. Dimorphism: male slimmer and much smaller than female. Food: flying insects. Specimen: No. 140 (female), from Cairns, North Queensland.

No common name *Cyrtophora hirta*
This species was named by L. Koch in 1872, from specimens sent from Bowen, Queensland. Its range extends from North Queensland, to the Blue Mountains, in New South Wales. Body length: male 5mm, female 10mm. Colour: as illustrated. Identification: by photograph. Egg-sac: plano-convex, 10mm in diameter, of greenish-white silk, with tufts of green silk attached to outer surface. Eggs: 0.8mm in diameter, pale cream in colour, 50 in number, non-glutinous. Dimorphism: male smaller and slimmer than female. Food: small insects. Specimen: No. 141 (female), from Cooktown. North Queensland.

Tailed Spider *Arachnura higginsi*
This unusual spider has an Australia-wide distribution, and is also found in Tasmania. It will sometimes curl its tail over its back if disturbed, and when it does this it is not unlike a scorpion. The orb web has a section missing from the centre top, in the shape of a "V". The spider sits in the centre of the web at all times, and when the eggs are laid, the egg-sacs are strung in a line down the centre of the web; the spider then sits on the last sac. The sacs are camouflaged with food remains and debris. The male of this species is a midget, and is often mistaken for a red-brown mite; thus he is likely to be overlooked by the student. The male does not have the long tail-like abdomen, and is usually found on the outskirts of the female's web.

Plate 36
139. *Cyrtophora crassipes* (female)
140. *Cyrtophora moluccensis* (female) with sac
141. *Cyrtophora hirta* (female) with sac
142. *Arachnura higginsi* (female)

139

140

141

142

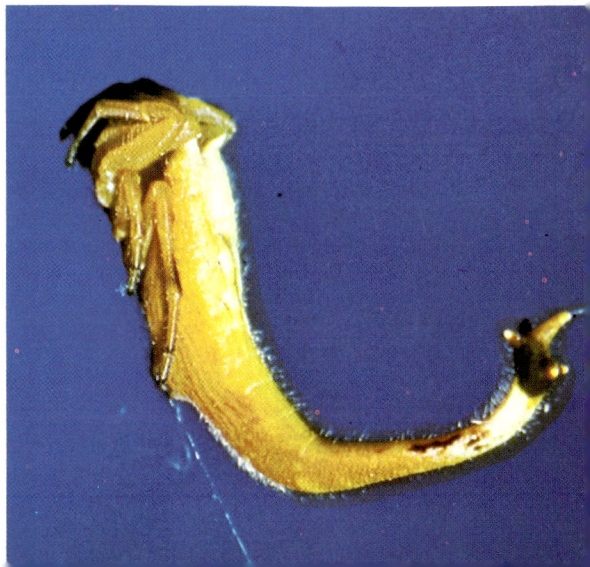

Tailed Spider *Arachnura higginsi*
The colour of this species varies considerably, and ranges from cream to brown. The web is usually built low down, and is mostly inclined, or even horizontal in some cases. The egg-sacs number up to eight. Body length: male 2mm, female 16mm. Colour: variable, from cream to brown (see Nos 142 and 143). Identification: by long abdomen with tiny horns on the end. Egg-sac: oval in shape, 5mm x 4mm, of tough, brown silk, with woolly appearance. Eggs: 0.8mm in diameter, of creamy colour, 50–60 in number, non-glutinous. Dimorphism: male very much smaller than female, and lacking a tail. Food: small flying insects. Specimens: Nos 142 and 143 (females), from Malabar, Sydney.

Tailed Spider *Arachnura feredayi*
This is another controversial species. Some authors are of the opinion that this spider is synonymous with *A. higginsi*, but after careful research the author is convinced they are separate species. L. Koch described this spider as *Epeira feredayi* in 1872, from specimens collected in New Zealand. The habits and web are similar to the preceding species. Body length: male 1.8mm, female 9mm. Colour: as illustrated, with little or no variation. Identification: by shorter abdomen, which lacks horns on the end. Egg-sac: oval in shape, 4mm x 3mm, of tough, brown silk, numbering up to five. Eggs: 0.7mm in diameter, opaque, of whitish colour, 30–45 in number, non-glutinous. Dimorphism: male much smaller than female, and lacking a tail. Food: small flying insects. Specimen: No. 144 (female), from North Ryde, Sydney.

No common name *Larinia phthisica*
This small species builds an orb web about 15cm in diameter, which is usually situated in tall grass close to the ground. It was described by L. Koch in 1871, under its present name. Its range is eastern Australia, from Queensland to Victoria, and it is fairly common around Sydney. Body length: male 6mm, female 7mm. Colour: as illustrated. Identification: by its size and the photograph. Egg-sac and eggs: unknown. Dimorphism: male almost as large as female. Food: small insects. Specimen: No. 145 (female), from Botany, Sydney.

No common name *Paraplectanoides crassipes*
A small spider, which was described by Keyserling in 1886. It builds a small orb web in low herbage, and is rather rare in New South Wales. The author is unfamiliar with its habits and breeding. Body length: male unknown, female 5mm. Colour: as illustrated. Identification: by its unusual carapace, and the photograph. Egg-sac and eggs: unknown, though one author records one egg-sac which contained 1,032 eggs. Dimorphism: unknown. Food: small insects, captured in orb web. Specimen: No. 146 (female), from Kurnell, Sydney.

Plate 37
143. *Arachnura higginsi* (female) with sacs
144. *Arachnura feredayi* (female) with sacs
145. *Larinia phthisica* (female)
146. *Paraplectanoides crassipes* (female)

143

144

145

146

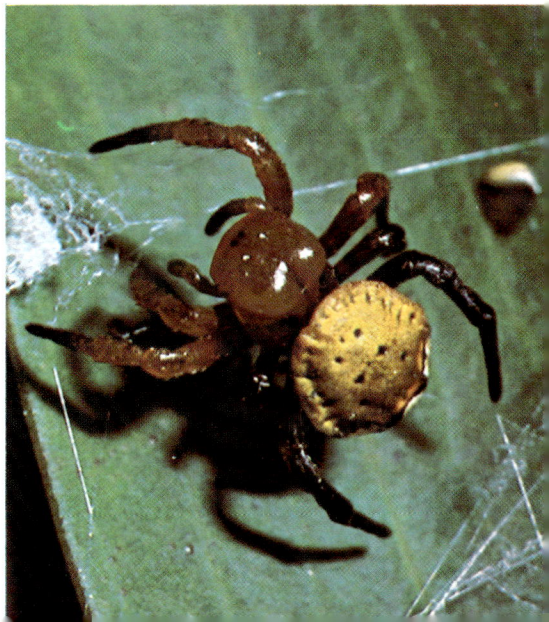

Three-lobed Spider *Cyclosa species*
The genus *Cyclosa* is a complex one, and like many other Australian genera, badly needs revisional work to clarify some of the species. In 1885, Urquhart described a species from New Zealand, as *Arachnura trilobata*. This spider was later placed in the genus *Cyclosa*, and it was found that it also occurred in Tasmania. When a similar species was later found in Australia, it was accepted as the same species, and referred to as such by many authors. After much revisional work on the Australian and New Zealand species, the present author found they are distinct species in habit, form and breeding habits. This means the Australian species (No. 147), is undescribed, and distinct from *Cyclosa trilobata* (No. 149). *Cyclosa* build a neat, orb web, usually in a low position, which may be recognised by a perpendicular line of food debris, running through the centre of the web. This line runs above and below the hub of the orb web, whereas in the web of *Arachnura* it terminates at the hub. The genus *Arachnura* place the egg-sacs in this line of debris, and *Cyclosa* place the egg-sacs outside the web. This unusual habit of the debris line in the web probably led to *C. trilobata* being described originally as *Arachnura trilobata*, by Urquhart. *Cyclosa sp.*, No. 147, varies considerably in colour on the abdomen. Some specimens have brilliant red on the dorsal surface, others have silver, some are almost entirely black. But as the author has stressed before, colour varies in many species of spiders. Body length: male 4mm, female 8mm. Colour: variable, from a silver stripe on the abdomen, to a bright red stripe, see Nos 147 and 148. Identification: by three lobes on posterior end of the abdomen. Egg-sac: oval in shape, 8.5mm x 6mm, orange-brown in colour, fastened to a grass stem. Eggs: 0.8mm in diameter, deep yellow-brown in colour, 45–60 in number, non-glutinous. Dimorphism:

male smaller than female, lobes on posterior end of abdomen smaller than those on female. Food: small insects, captured in orb web. Specimens: Nos 147 and 148 (females), from Cordeaux Dam, New South Wales.

Three-lobed Spider *Cyclosa trilobata*
This is the New Zealand species, shown to check with the Australian species. The lobes on the end of the abdomen are smaller and thicker, and the colours are not so bright, though there is a similarity in the general shape. Body length: male 5mm, female 9mm. Colour: as illustrated. Identification: by photograph. Egg-sac: conical in shape, sienna brown in colour, of smooth, papery texture on outer surface, 12mm long x 6.5mm high, fastened to a twig. Eggs: 0.9mm in diameter, dirty yellow in colour, 48 and 56 respectively in the two sacs examined. Dimorphism: male smaller than female. Food: probably small flying insects. Specimen: No. 149 (female), from Taupo, New Zealand.

Plate 38
147. *Cyclosa species* (female) with sac
148. *Cyclosa species* (female) with sac
149. *Cyclosa trilobata* (female) with sac
150. Sacs of Nos 147, 148 and 149 for comparison

147

148

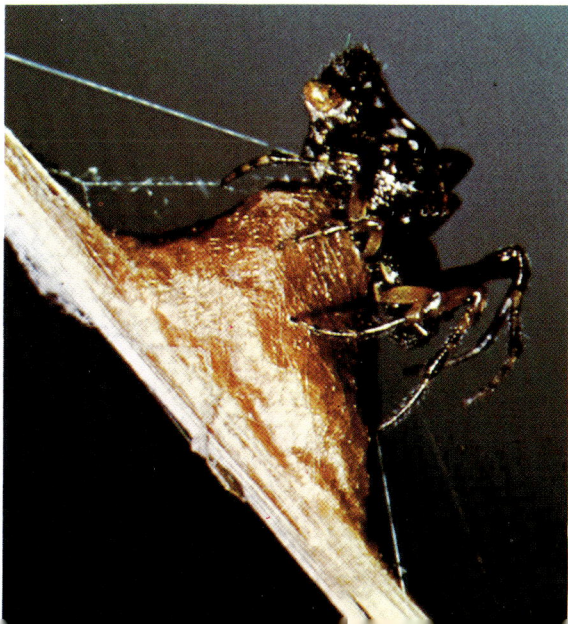

149

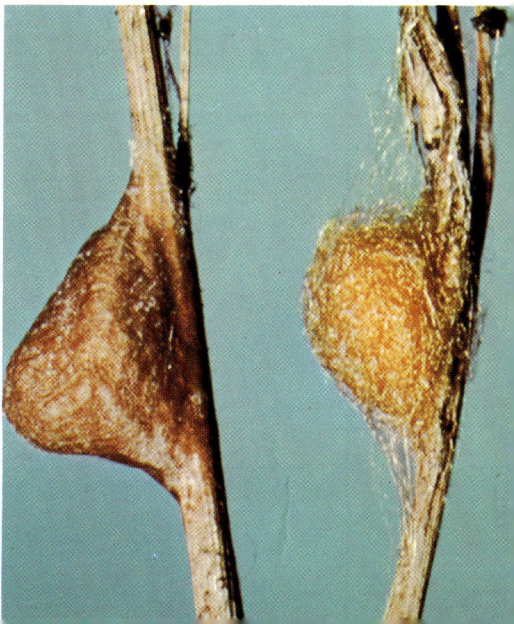

150

Orb-weaving Spider *Araneus psittacinus*

The orb-weaving spiders are well-known to most householders, for their habits of building webs across passageways and yards in suburban homes. The genus *Araneus* is one of the largest in Australia, over 100 species having been recorded. They vary in size from midgets a few millimetres in body length to giants with bodies over 3.5cm in length. *A. psittacinus* is one of the small species, and was included for its beautiful body-colours. It is usually found in heavy timber or semi-rain-forest, though one or two specimens have been collected from coastal scrub. Body length: male unknown, female 5mm. Colour: as illustrated. Identification: by photograph. Egg-sac: unknown, as are eggs. Dimorphism: male smaller and slimmer than female. Food: small insects. Specimen: No. 151 (female), from Royal National Park, Audley, Sydney.

Orb-weaving Spider *Araneus pustulosa*

This is a very widespread species, being found in Tasmania, all over Australia, New Zealand, and many of the Pacific Islands. Body length: male 7–8mm, female 10–15mm. Colour: variable, from yellow-brown to black. Identification: by five small tubercules on posterior end of the abdomen, and photograph. Egg-sac: about 15mm long x 10mm wide, oval in shape, of brown, woolly silk, with green tufts attached to outer surface. Eggs: unknown. Dimorphism: male smaller and slimmer than female, with heavy spining on legs one and two. Food: a wide variety of insects, captured in its orb web. Specimen: No. 152 (female), from Ku-ring-gai Chase, Sydney.

Enamelled Spider *Araneus bradleyi*

Another species which is variable in colour, but which is easily identified by the enamelled appearance of the body. The orb web is built fairly low down, and is usually attached to low bushes and grass. The spider sits in the centre of the web at night and hides in the surrounds during daylight hours. Body length: male 8–9mm, female 14–18mm. Identification: by enamelled appearance, and photograph. Colour: variable, from azure blue to the colours illustrated. Egg-sac; round in shape, flat on the bottom where it is fastened down, of red-brown silk, with a woolly appearance. Eggs: golden yellow in colour, 1mm in diameter, in a glutinous mass. Dimorphism: male smaller and slimmer, though similar in appearance. Food: small flying insects. Specimen: No. 153 (female), from Royal National Park, Audley, Sydney.

Orb-weaving Spider *Araneus transmarinus*

Sometimes called the Garden Spider, this is a large species, and is found in Queensland, New South Wales, and Victoria. This spider is commonly found in yards, and it does a lot of good in keeping down insect pests; it is not poisonous, and has been observed to capture fifty moths in one night. Body length: male 15–17mm, female 20–25mm. Identification: by illustration. Colour: from light grey to black. Egg-sac: oval, up to 3cm x 2cm, grey to green in colour. Eggs: 1mm in diameter, cream in colour, several hundred in number. Dimorphism: male smaller than female. Food: insects. Specimen: No. 154 (female), from Botany, Sydney.

Plate 39
151. *Araneus psittacinus* (female)
152. *Araneus pustulosa* (female)
153. *Araneus bradleyi* (female)
154. *Araneus transmarinus* (female)

151

152

153

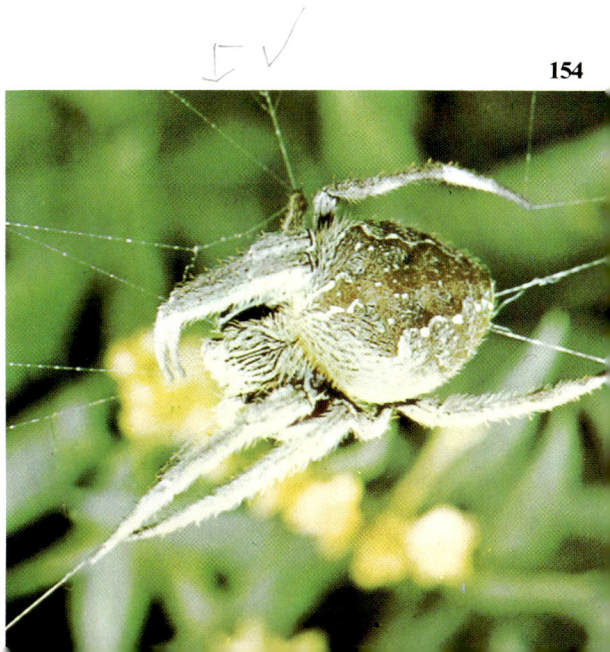

154

No common name *Carepalxis coronata*

This species is the largest of the genus *Carepalxis*, and builds a beautiful orb web 60cm in diameter. The spiral threads are so close together, that the orb looks like a solid sheet of web. The spider inhabits semi-rain-forest, and its range is from Queensland to Sydney. It is purely nocturnal in habits, building the orb web after darkness has fallen. It sits head-down in the centre of the web until just before dawn, then it cuts the web down and hides in the surrounding bushes. Body length: male unknown, female 13.5mm. Colour: as illustrated. Identification: by photograph. Egg-sac and eggs: unknown. Dimorphism: male probably smaller than female. Food: very small flying insects, which inhabit the leaf litter in the rain-forest. Specimen: No. 155 (female), from Royal National Park, Audley, Sydney.

No common name *Carepalxis poweri*

A much smaller species, which was described by W. Rainbow in 1915, from a specimen collected at Narrabeen, Sydney, by Master C. D. Power. This spider also builds an orb web, and it too, has very closely arranged spiral threads. Body length: male unknown, female 5mm. Colour: as illustrated. Identification: by photograph. Egg-sac and egg: unknown. Dimorphism: male probably smaller than female. Food: minute flying insects. Specimen: No. 156 (female), from Royal National Park, Audley, Sydney.

No common name *Poltys mammeatus*

This remarkable genus contains some of our weirdly-shaped spiders. The orb webs built by *Poltys* are even finer and more closely spun than those made by the previous genus. The webs are only built after dark, and cut down again before daylight. The spiders then fold their legs tightly to their bodies, and sit on a twig during daylight hours. They are never found on growing trees, only on dead limbs, and their colour always matches the twig they sit on—so much so that they cannot be detected at a few inches. This species was described by Keyserling in 1886; its range is from Queensland to at least Sydney. Body length: male 4mm, female 9mm. Colour: as illustrated. Identification: by its unusual shape, and photograph. Egg-sac: unknown to the author, as are the eggs. Dimorphism: male smaller, and abdomen not so high as that of the female. Food: small flying insects. Specimen: No. 157 (female), from Ku-ring-gai Chase, Sydney.

No common name *Poltys laciniosus*

Similar in habits to *P. mammeatus*, and fairly common in the Sydney area. Body length: male 4.2mm, female 10mm. Colour: as illustrated. Identification: by two tuberculate shoulders on anterior end of abdomen, and photograph. Egg-sac and eggs: unknown. Dimorphism: male smaller than female. Food: small flying insects. Specimen: No. 158 (female), from Ku-ring-gai Chase, Sydney.

Plate 40
155. *Carepalxis coronata* (female)
156. *Carepalxis poweri* (female)
157. *Poltys mammeatus* (female)
158. *Poltys laciniosus* (female)

155

156

157

158

Six-spined Spider *Gasteracantha minax*
Thorell named this species in 1859. Then in 1871 L. Koch named an all-black species as *G. lugubris*, and another species which was black on top but patterned underneath as *G. astrigera*. Hogg later named these two as varieties of *G. minax*. After studying hundreds of specimens, both male and female, the present author is convinced that *G. lugubris* is a melanic form, and *G. astrigera* is a semi-melanic form, of *Gasteracantha minax*. Of the hundreds of males observed in their habitat, all were the normal form, and were mating with normal females, all-black females, and semi-black females; no black or semi-black males were found. *Gasteracantha minax* is found in all States and Tasmania. They are often found in aggregates, with some webs overlapping others. The orb web is usually built between low bushes, or in tall grass; the spider sits in the hub of the orb. The radial strands of the web often have small, fluffy balls of white silk at intervals of about 3.5cm. Body length: male 3.2mm, female 7–10mm. Colour: as illustrated. Identification: by photograph. Egg-sac: variable in shape, usually attached to a twig on the outskirts of the web. About 25mm in length, thicker in the centre, tapering towards the ends, of red-brown silk, with darker binding threads. Eggs: 0.8mm in diameter, deep yellow in colour, 130–150 in number, non-glutinous. Dimorphism: male much smaller than female, spines on male blunter. Food: small insects. Specimens: No. 159 (female), No. 160 (male and female), from Malabar, Sydney.

Spiny Spider *Gasteracantha fornicata*
A spectacular spider, first described by Thorell from specimens collected in Java. It is now recorded from North Queensland, where it is not uncommon. Like the previous species, it builds an orb web, and sits in the hub of the orb. All species of *Gastera-cantha* have hard bodies, and this seems to deter birds from attacking them. Body length: male unknown, though probably tiny. Colour: as illustrated. Identification: by photograph and colour pattern. Egg-sac: oval in shape, lime-green in colour, 13mm x 10mm, of basket-like silk. Eggs: 0.6mm in diameter, pale lemon-yellow in colour, 183 in number, non-glutinous. Dimorphism: unknown. Food: small insects. Specimen: No. 161 (female), from Cairns, North Queensland.

Spiny Spider *Gasteracantha sacerdotalis*
L. Koch described this species in 1871, from specimens collected at Bowen, North Queensland; it is also found in the Pelew Islands. The orb web is built between low bushes and in tall grass. Body length: male 2.5mm, female 6–7mm. Colour: as illustrated. Identification: by shorter spines, and photograph. Egg-sac and eggs: unknown. Dimorphism: male much smaller than female. Food: small insects. Specimen: No. 162 (female), from Cairns, North Queensland.

Plate 41
159. *Gasteracantha minax* (female)
160. *Gasteracantha minax* (male and female) mating
161. *Gasteracantha fornicata* (female) with sac
162. *Gasteracantha sacerdotalis* (female)

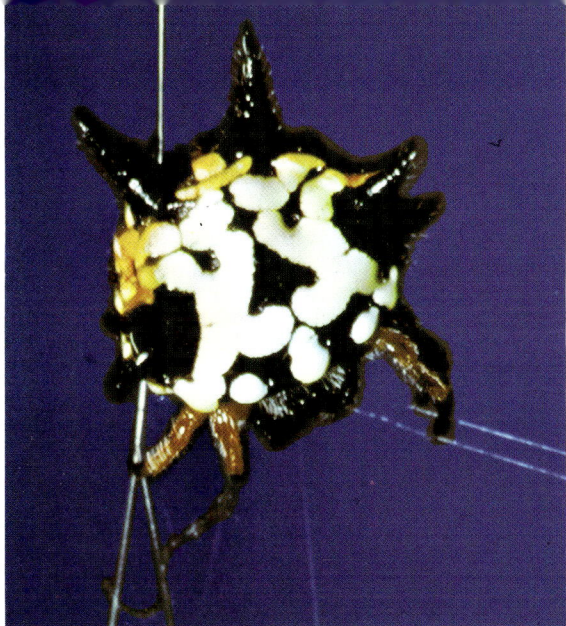

159

160

161

162

Bolas Spider *Dicrostichus furcatus*
A remarkable spider, which builds no web-snare, but captures its food by casting a bolas. The bolas is comprised of a silken thread, with a sticky globule attached to the end of it. The spider hangs head-down from a few strands of strong silk, firmly held by legs three and four. Legs one and two are extended, a silken thread coming from the spinnerets to the tip of leg two, then hanging for about 4cm, with the sticky globule on the end of it. In this position the spider jerks its body up and down, swinging the bolas in a circle each time it jerks its body. When a moth flies within a reasonable distance, the spider releases the thread from the tip of leg two, at the same time playing out silk from the spinnerets. As it releases the thread, the spider flicks leg two in the direction of the moth, and the aim is quite accurate.

Of the four instances witnessed by the author, all were successful, and no moths escaped. Once the bolas hits the moth, it becomes entangled, and is then wound up to the spider—and devoured after being wrapped in silk. Body length: male unknown, female 12mm. Colour: as illustrated. Identification: by egg-sacs when present, and photograph. Egg-sac: spindle-shaped, of brown, papery silk, up to 5.5cm long, 1.5cm wide at the widest point, numbering up to 5. Eggs: 1mm in diameter, bright yellow in colour, 178 in number, in a glutinous ball. Dimorphism: unknown. Food: moths. Specimens: Nos 163 and 164 (females), from Mt Druitt, New South Wales.

Bolas Spider *Ordgarius monstrosus*
This tropical species was described by Keyserling in 1886, and apparently it ended there, for the author can find no further description of this spider since Keyserling's work. The habits of this species are the same as the preceding species, but the egg-sacs are different in shape. Body length: male unknown, female 10mm. Colour: as illustrated. Identification: by three horny spines on the dorsal surface of the carapace, and the photograph. Egg-sac: roughly spherical, with a tail on the top, of rich brown, papery silk, five or six small, pointed protuberances spread around the centre of the sac. Sac suspended by the tail. Eggs: 1mm in diameter, deep red in colour, 120 in number. Young hatch in September. Dimorphism: unknown. Food: moths. Specimens: Nos 165 and 166 (females), from Cairns, North Queensland. *Note:* Similar species to these are found in Africa and America. One American species, *Mastophora bisaccata*, builds identical egg-sacs to *Ordgarius monstrosus*, and when it was first described, it was also placed in the genus *Ordgarius*. It has since been changed to *Mastophora*.

Plate 42
163. *Dicrostichus furcatus* (female)
164. *Dicrostichus furcatus* (female) with sacs
165. *Ordgarius monstrosus* (female)
166. *Ordgarius monstrosus* (female) with sacs

163

164

165

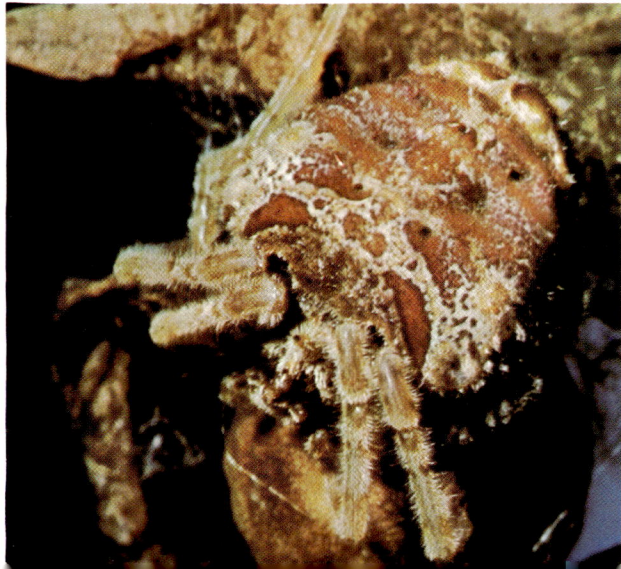

166

No common name *Dolophones maximus*

An unusual genus of spiders, in which the species have bodies which are concave on the ventral surface. This enables the spiders to wrap their bodies around a twig during the day, thus avoiding detection. Though it is not generally known, these spiders build orb webs at night, and cut them down before first light in the morning. The webs are similar to those of *Carepalxis* and *Poltys*, very closely spun in the spiral threads. *D. maximus* was described by Hogg in 1900, under its present name. Body length: male unknown, female 6mm. Colour: as illustrated. Identification: by photograph. Egg-sac and eggs: unknown. Dimorphism: male probably smaller than female. Food: small insects. Specimen: No. 167 (female), from Botany, Sydney.

No common name *Dolophones conifera*

This species has a wide distribution, being found in Queensland, New South Wales, Victoria, and Western Australia. Like all *Dolophones*, the colour of this species usually matches the tree on which it is found, and it is difficult to see the spider during daylight hours even at a few inches, when it is wrapped around a twig. Body length: male 8mm, female 10mm. Colour: variable. Identification: by photograph. Egg-sac: of brown, woolly silk, 11mm in diameter, wrapped around a twig. Eggs: 1mm in diameter, of creamy colour, 50 in number, non-glutinous. Dimorphism: male slightly smaller than female, longer in the legs. Food: small insects. Specimen: No. 168 (female), from Roseville, Sydney.

No common name *Dolophones pilosa*

This species was described by L. Koch in 1886 as *Tholia pilosa*, and is similar in habit to the two preceding species. Its range is from Queensland to Victoria. Body length: male 5.4mm, female 7mm. Colour: variable. Identification: by its hairy appearance and photograph. Egg-sac and eggs: unknown. Dimorphism: male slightly smaller, and longer in the legs than female. Food: small insects. Specimen: No. 169 (female), from Mt Victoria, New South Wales.

No common name *Dolophones nasalis*

Described by Butler in 1876, this species has a nose-like protuberance on the posterior end of its abdomen. It is found in Queensland and New South Wales. Body length: male unknown, female 10mm. Colour: as illustrated. Identification: by nose-like protuberance on end of abdomen. Egg-sac: domed, wrapped on a twig, 8mm in diameter, with brown, woolly appearance on outside. Eggs: 0.8mm in diameter, opaque, cream in colour, with white frosty appearance on outer surface, 59 in number, in a glutinous ball. Dimorphism: male slightly smaller than female. Food: small insects. Specimen: No. 170 (female), from Yagoona, Sydney.

Plate 43
167. *Dolophones maximus* (female)
168. *Dolophones conifera* (female) with sac
169. *Dolophones pilosa* (female)
170. *Dolophones nasalis* (female) with sac

167

168

169

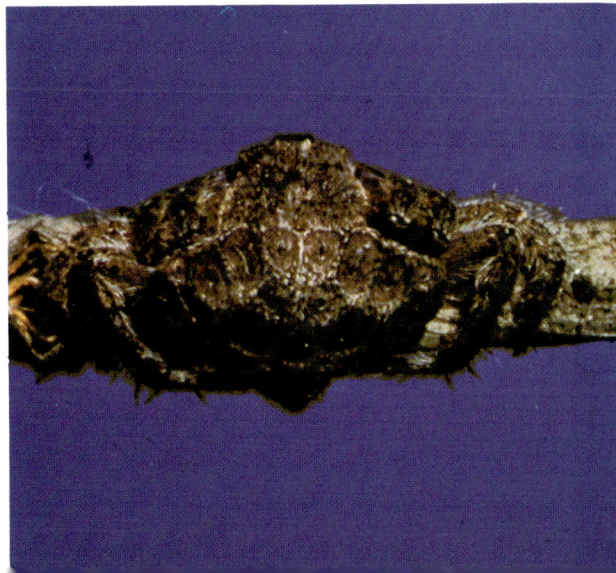

170

Triangular Spider *Arcys cornutus*
Though tiny spiders, the members of this genus are among the most colourful in Australia, and the unusual body-shape is an added attraction to students. The members of this genus do not build web-snares, but capture their prey by grasping it with legs one and two, which are heavily spined. This species was named by L. Koch in 1871, under its present name, and it is found in Queensland and New South Wales. Body length: male unknown, female 6mm. Colour: as illustrated. Identification: by photograph. Egg-sac and eggs: unknown. Dimorphism: male probably slimmer and slightly smaller than female. Food: small insects. Specimen: No. 171 (female), from Boronia Park, Sydney.

Triangular Spider *Arcys alatus*
Though the common name Triangular Spider has been given to the genus *Arcys*, it would not apply to this species. The author is of the opinion that this spider should be in the genus *Archemorus*, and it will probably be placed in it at a later date. The female is undescribed, the male having been described by Keyserling in 1890. Body length: male 5mm, female 6mm. Colour: variable, from grey to cream. Identification: by its unusual shape, and photograph. Egg-sac and eggs: unknown. Dimorphism: male almost equal in length with female, though slightly slimmer. Food: small insects. Specimens: Nos 172 (male) and 173 (female), from Royal National Park, Audley, Sydney.

Triangular Spider *Arcys lancearius*
This is another beautiful spider, and probably the commonest species of the genus, though these spiders are never found in quantity anywhere. There is also a melanic, or black form of this species (No. 176). To the author's knowledge, the egg-sacs of this genus have never been recorded, and their life histories and habits are unknown. The egg-sac is built in January–February, the young hatching in about five weeks. After that, nothing is known of their lives. Body length: male 5.5mm, female 7–8mm. Colour: as illustrated. Identification: by photograph, and heart-shaped body. Egg-sac: spherical, 8mm in diameter, deep pink-cream in colour, with a basket-like outer covering of lighter coloured threads. The sac is suspended by strong threads, that pictured was found under a fern frond. Eggs: 0.7mm in diameter, yellow in colour, 72 in number, in a glutinous ball. Dimorphism: male smaller than female. Food: small insects. Specimen: No. 174 (female), from Turramurra, Sydney.

Plate 44
171. *Arcys cornutus* (female)
172. *Arcys alatus* (male)
173. *Arcys alatus* (female)
174. *Arcys lancearius* (female)

171

172

173

174

Triangular Spider *Arcys clavatus*
This is a colourful species with a slightly different-shaped abdomen. This species is easily distinguishable from *A. lancearius* by its longer abdomen, and the unusual colour-pattern. Whereas *A. lancearius* is found in Queensland, New South Wales, Victoria, and Tasmania, this species is restricted to New South Wales and Victoria. Once again, its life habits are a closed book, for this species is only found on odd occasions. The fact that the members of this genus do not build web-snares makes the spiders much more difficult to locate. Even when they are located, they are continually on the move by playing out a line of silk until it reaches another tree or bush. Once it is secured, they move along it to the next tree. This makes continued study impossible. In New South Wales this species has a wide distribution, having been observed just about all over the State. Body length: male 4mm, female 6mm. Colour: variable, some specimens being much darker than others. Identification: by long abdomen, and colour pattern. Egg-sac: pear-shaped, 10mm long, 5mm wide at the bottom, very fine lacework of pale cream silk on outer covering, suspended by strong threads at the top. Eggs: 0.8mm in diameter, yellow in colour, 48 in number, in a glutinous ball. Dimorphism: male smaller and slimmer than female. Food: small insects. Specimens: No. 175 (female), from Helensburgh, New South Wales; No. 178 (female), from Mt Victoria, New South Wales.

Triangular Spider *Arcys lancearius*
This is the first record of melanism in this genus, so is worthy of inclusion. The semi-melanic spider pictured was collected among ferns which were dead and partly burned. A short distance away, normal forms were collected from live ferns. Melanism would appear to be very prevalent among Australian spiders, probably due to our high bush fire rate. Normal forms would find it hard to survive in a burned-out area, as their colour would give their position away to predators. Specimen: No. 176 (female), from Gosford, New South Wales.

Triangular Spider *Arcys lancearius*
As this photograph and No. 178 are the first records of egg-sacs in this genus, and as those of *A. lancearius* and *A. clavatus* differ in build and texture, the author felt they should be shown. In this way, some student may follow on, and fill in the gaps in this unusual genus's life history. It seems strange that though the genus has been known for almost 100 years, nothing is known of its ways or habits. This would appear to be a small genus, as there are only five described species, and the last of these was named in 1908. This was a species from Western Australia, *A. nitidiceps*. The other four species were described last century. Specimens: No. 177 (female), from Gosford, New South Wales; No. 178 (female), from Mt. Victoria, New South Wales.

Plate 45
175. *Arcys clavatus* (female)
176. *Arcys lancearius* (female) melanic form
177. *Arcys lancearius* (female) with sac
178. *Arcys clavatus* (female) with sac

175

176

177

178

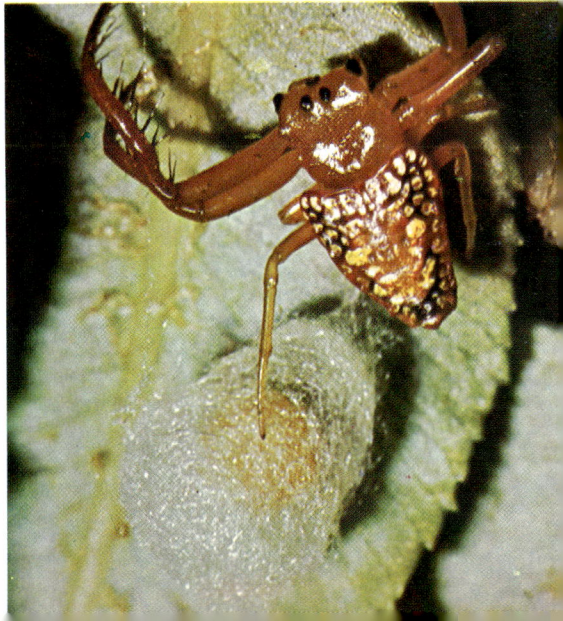

No common name *Archemorus simsoni*

Many students have difficulty in separating the genera *Arcys* and *Archemorus*. When Simon erected the genus *Archemorus* in 1892, he used a key based on the eyes and the width of the abdomen. He stated that if the posterior eyes of the median group were raised on tubercules, and the abdomen was wider than it was long, the spider belonged to the genus *Archemorus*. If these spiders are studied in life, it is simple to distinguish between the two genera. *Archemorus* sit with legs one and two folded tightly to the body, while *Arcys* sit with legs one and two stretched out diagonally from the front of the body.

There are only three species of this genus described from Australia, but many more await discovery, for the author has twelve undescribed species awaiting descriptions; the Australian Museum has another. Body length: male 5mm, female 7mm. Colour: as illustrated. Identification: by three horny tubercules on dorsal surface of the abdomen, the anterior one being the largest. Egg-sac: spherical, with fluffy, white silk covering the outer surface and a tail at the top, by which the sac is suspended. Eggs: 0.6mm in diameter, opaque, off-white in colour, 46 in number, non-glutinous. Dimorphism: male slightly smaller, longer in the legs, and slimmer than female. Food: small insects, and occasionally small spiders. Specimens: No. 179 (male and female), No. 180 (female), from Minnamurra Falls Reserve, Kiama, New South Wales.

No common name *Archemorus species*

An undescribed species, which strangely enough has only been collected off one species of tree, the Brown Beech, *Pennantia cunninghamii*. This is a semi-rain-forest species, and so far, the male has not been collected. Body length: male unknown, female 4.5mm. Colour: as illustrated. Identification: by photograph. Egg-sac and eggs: unknown. Dimorphism: unknown. Food: tiny insects. Specimen: No. 181 (female), from Minnamurra Falls Reserve, Kiama, New South Wales.

No common name *Neoarchemorus speechleyi*

The male and female of this small spider were collected by Mr A. E. Speechley, and passed on to the author for classification. It was an undescribed species, and would not fit into any known genera, so a new genus was erected for it in 1967 by the author. Body length: male 4.2mm, female 5mm. Colour: as illustrated. Identification: by photograph. Egg-sac: spherical, 5mm in diameter, with several thin strips of fluffy silk running edgewise around the sac, and a tail at the top, by which the sac is suspended; sac white. Eggs: 0.5mm in diameter, opaque, off-white in colour, 54 in number, non-glutinous. Dimorphism: male smaller and thinner than female. Food: small insects. Specimen: No. 182 (female), from Royal National Park, Audley, Sydney.

Plate 46
179. *Archemorus simsoni* (male and female)
180. *Archemorus simsoni* (female) with sac
181. *Archemorus species* (female)
182. *Neoarchemorus speechleyi* (female)

179

180

181

182

FAMILY HERSILIIDAE

No common name *Tama fickerti*

The spiders of this genus are easily identified by the two long spinnerets which protrude past the posterior end of the abdomen. Described by L. Koch in 1876 as *Chalinura fickerti*, this species is one of four members of the genus found in Australia. *T. fickerti* is a New South Wales species, but has a widespread distribution in this State. This is another genus in which melanism is prevalent, due to the spiders inhabiting the outer bark of trees. If they were not able to adopt this dark form, they would be too obvious to predators when they ballooned into an area after a fire. Body length: male 4mm, female 7mm. Colour: variable, from grey through browns to black. Identification: by two long spinnerets protruding from posterior end of abdomen. Egg-sac: an oval disc, 10mm x 7mm, camouflaged to match the bark. Eggs: 0.6mm in diameter, a translucent, off-white colour, 35–50 in number, non-glutinous. Dimorphism: male smaller, slimmer, and with longer legs than female. Food: small bark-dwelling insects and other spiders. Specimens: Nos 183 and 184 (females), from North Ryde, Sydney.

FAMILY OXYOPIDAE

Lynx Spider *Oxyopes elegans*

Oxyopes are small spiders which build no web-snare. Instead they are adept jumpers, and use this skill to great advantage in capturing food. Usually found on grass or low herbage, these spiders may be identified by the long spines which stand out at right angles to the legs. Described by L. Koch in 1878 under its present name, this species ranges from Queensland, right through New South Wales. Body length: male 4mm, female 6mm. Colour: as illustrated. Identification: by spines on the legs, and photograph. Egg-sac: oval in shape, of very white silk, usually in grass, or under a leaf. Eggs: 0.6mm in diameter, pale cream in colour, 35–45 in number, non-glutinous. Dimorphism: male smaller and much slimmer than female. Food: small insects. Specimen: No. 185 (female), from Botany, Sydney.

FAMILY AGELENIDAE

Platform Spider *Corasoides australis*

This unusual spider digs a burrow up to 16cm deep, from which rises a silken tube 6cm long. This tube extends into a silken sheet, widening from 2cm at the tube, to about 22cm at the other end. The platform, or sheet, is supported by a labyrinth of guy threads. Insects hitting these threads are knocked down on to the platform, on which the spider runs. Body length: male 9mm, female 15mm. Colour: as illustrated. Identification: by photograph, and the platform in the web. Egg-sac: spherical or nearly so, 14mm in diameter, made of silk and soil bound together, inner sac of white, papery silk. Eggs: 1mm in diameter, of creamy colour, 40–55 in number, non-glutinous. Dimorphism: male smaller and slimmer than female. Food: insects. Specimen: No. 186 (male), from Royal National Park, Audley, Sydney.

Plate 47
183. *Tama fickerti* (female)
184. *Tama fickerti* (female) melanic form
185. *Oxyopes elegans* (female) with sac
186. *Corasoides australis* (male)

183

184

185

186

FAMILY ZODARIIDAE

No common name *Storena formosa*
Like many other Australian spiders, the members of this genus are vagrants, and build no web-snare. They may be found in rotten logs, under stones or debris, or just wandering about. As is the case with many other genera and species, very little is known of the private lives of these spiders. A few species build shallow burrows, some place a palisade of twigs or debris around the burrow entrance. Thorell described this species under its present name; L. Koch later described it under *Habronestes formosus*, and this becomes a synonym of *Storena formosa*, for Thorell's description was in 1870, Koch's in 1872. Those species which do not dig a burrow usually dig a depression for the egg-sac, and all females remain with the egg-sac once it is built. Body length: male 11mm, female 16mm. Colour: as illustrated. Identification: by colour-pattern of the body. Egg-sac and eggs: unknown. Dimorphism: male smaller and slimmer than female. Food: ground-dwelling insects. Specimens: No. 187 (male), from Moama, New South Wales; No. 188 (female), from Jenolan Caves, New South Wales.

No common name *Storena graeffei*
This species is probably the largest of this genus, for though the author is unfamiliar with the female, the male is a giant among Storenas. Body length: male 13mm, female unknown. Colour: as illustrated. Identification: by photograph. Egg-sac and eggs: unknown. Dimorphism: female probably slightly larger than the male. Food: ground-dwelling insects. Specimen: No. 189 (male), from Narromine, New South Wales.

FAMILY LYCOSIDAE

Wolf Spider *Geolycosa pictiventris*
The wolf spiders are well-known in Australia, and this country has the greatest number of representatives of any country in the world. Most of the species were described by L. Koch in the 1870s, and have stood as such since. In 1961, Gisela Rack completed a survery of L. Koch's type specimens in the Hamburg Museum, Germany, where they are lodged. Many species were placed in other genera, but this author feels more work should be done on this family, and is loath to change the established names until such time as this work is done. However, to keep this book up to date, the new names will be given in brackets after the old one. Body length: male 10mm, female 13mm. Colour: as illustrated. Identification: by body pattern, and photograph. Egg-sac: spherical, of grey-brown colour, 6mm in diameter. Eggs: unknown. Dimorphism: male slimmer, and smaller than female. Food: small ground-dwelling insects, and other spiders. Specimen: No. 190 (female), from Botany, Sydney.

Plate 48
187. *Storena formosa* (male)
188. *Storena formosa* (female)
189. *Storena graeffei* (male)
190. *Geolycosa pictiventris* (female)

187

188

189

190

Wolf Spider *Lycosa subligata (Hogna subligata)*
This beautiful species inhabits the drier regions of
the continent, and its colouring is such that it
harmonises with the red soil. It was described by
L. Koch in 1877 as *Pirata subligatus*, but was later
found to belong to *Lycosa*. Body length: male
unknown, female 14mm. Colour: as illustrated,
though it would probably vary in different districts.
Identification: by the photograph. Egg-sac and
eggs: unknown. Dimorphism: male probably
smaller and slimmer. Food: ground-dwelling insects and other spiders. Specimen: No. 191 (female),
from Cobar, New South Wales.

Wolf Spider *Trochosa exculta (Allohogna exculta)*
Another beautiful species of which very little is
known, for this is a rare spider. L. Koch described
the species in 1877, under its present name, from
specimens collected at Gayndah, North Queensland. This specimen was collected from south of
Sydney, so it extends the range considerably. Body
length: male unknown, female 12mm. Colour: as
illustrated. Identification: by the body pattern, and
the photograph. Egg-sac and eggs: unknown.
Dimorphism: male probably smaller and slimmer
than female. Food: small ground-dwelling insects.
Specimen: No. 192 (female), from Wollongong,
New South Wales.

Wolf Spider *Geolycosa serrata*
Though a smaller species than most Lycosids, this
is a remarkable species for its habit of placing a
palisade at the burrow entrance. The palisades used
by this genus vary from species to species, and the
workmanship which goes into the building of them,
has to be seen to be believed. Some species build a
collar of leaves and debris above ground level,
others use a leaf or stone as a lid for the burrow
which is not hinged, but sealed on the under-surface.

Others forage on the seashore, and use shells and
jetsam for a home, while other species build palisades of stones, rabbit dung, or twigs. One large
species lives above the snowline on Mount
Kosciusko, where it is buried beneath snow for
several months of the year. Another species lives
in swamps, and can run across water quite freely.
There is much work to be done on this large and
complex genus and its allied genera.

This species is found in open coastal scrub,
usually in sandy conditions. Body length: male
9mm, female 12mm. Colour: as illustrated. Identification: by photograph, and palisade at entrance
to burrow. Egg-sac: spherical, 6mm in diameter, of
grey silk, seamed around the centre, carried by the
female. Eggs: 1mm in diameter, pale yellow in
colour, 50 in number, non-glutinous. Dimorphism:
male slimmer, and smaller than the female. Food:
ground-dwelling insects. Specimens: Nos 193 and
194 (female and palisade), from Malabar, Sydney.

Plate 49
191. *Lycosa subligata (Hogna subligata)* (female)
192. *Trochosa exculta (Allohogna exculta)* (female)
193. *Geolycosa serrata* (female)
194. *Geolycosa serrata* (palisade)

191

192

193

194

Wolf Spider *Lycosa simsoni*

This species has a lid to its burrow, but unlike the trap-door spiders, there is no hinge to the lid, and the spider usually does not build the lid. A leaf, stone, piece of bark, or similar article is used, although on rare occasions, this spider will build a lid from soil and silk if no loose object is available. To open the lid, the spider lays it to one side of the burrow entrance; to close it, it pulls the lid over, and seals it to the entrance with silk. Body length: male 11–13mm, female 15–16mm. Colour: as illustrated. Identification: by photograph, and lid on burrow. Egg-sac: spherical, or nearly so, 8mm in diameter, of grey silk, seamed around the centre, carried by the female attached to the spinnerets. Eggs: 1mm in diameter, off-white in colour, 50–60 in number, non-glutinous. Dimorphism: male slimmer and smaller than female. Food: insects. Specimen: No. 195 (female), from Springwood, New South Wales.

Wolf Spider *Lycosa furcillata (Allocosa furcillata)*

An eastern species which is confined to Queensland and New South Wales. It was described by L. Koch in 1867, under its present name. This species is common in the suburbs of Sydney, and is often seen running around on lawns. Body length: male 9mm, female 13mm. Colour: as illustrated. Identification: by photograph, and dorsal pattern on the abdomen. Egg-sac: spherical, grey in colour, 6mm in diameter, carried by the female attached to the spinnerets. Eggs: 0.8mm in diameter, pale cream in colour, 45–60 in number. Dimorphism: male smaller in the body, and slimmer than female. Food: ground-dwelling insects. Specimen: No. 196 (female), from Botany, Sydney.

Wolf Spider *Lycosa palabunda (Allocosa palabunda)*

A widespread eastern species which is found in Queensland, New South Wales, and many South Sea Islands. It was described by L. Koch in 1877, under its present name. It is fairly common throughout New South Wales, particularly in dead grass and low coastal scrub. This species digs a shallow burrow, with no adornments or lid, which is usually in open ground, but adjacent to dead grass or debris. Body length: male 8mm, female up to 16mm. Colour: as illustrated, though it could vary according to the soil in a particular area. Identification: by the photograph, and the dorsal pattern on the abdomen. Egg-sac: spherical, or nearly so, 10mm in diameter, of light blue, papery silk, seamed around the centre. Eggs: 1.1mm in diameter, of a dusty, pale brown colour, 65 in number, non-glutinous. Dimorphism: male smaller than female, but as long in the legs. Food: ground-dwelling insects, and other spiders. Specimens: Nos 197 and 198 (females), from Ryde, Sydney.

Note: The simple identification features mentioned in the text are for the use of laymen only. The genitalia of spiders are the positive means by which a species is determined. This requires a microscope and other scientific equipment, as used by the author.

Plate 50
195. *Lycosa simsoni* (female)
196. *Lycosa furcillata (Allocosa furcillata)* (female)
197. *Lycosa palabunda (Allocosa palabunda)* (female) with sac
198. *Lycosa palabunda (Allocosa palabunda)* (female) with young

195

196

197

198

INDEX